Pine Bluff / Jefferson
Library

200 East 8th Ave
Pine Bluff, Arkansas
pinebluefflibrary.org

E. M. Fors

D0859820

Martial Rose

New York

Published 1971 by ARCO PUBLISHING COMPANY, Inc.
219 Park Avenue South, New York, N.Y. 10003
Copyright © Martial Rose,
All Rights Reserved
Library of Congress Catalog Number 77-123550
Printed in the United States of America

/57669

R
823.912
R797E

Arco Literary Critiques

Of recent years, the ordinary man who reads for pleasure has been gradually excluded from that great debate in which every intelligent reader of the classics takes part. There are two reasons for this: first, so much criticism floods from the world's presses that no one but a scholar living entirely among books can hope to read it all; and second, the critics and analysts, mostly academics, use a language that only their fellows in the same discipline can understand.

Consequently criticism, which should be as 'inevitable as breathing'—an activity for which we are all qualified—has become the private field of a few warring factions who shout their unintelligible battle cries to each other but make little communication to the common man.

Arco Literary Critiques aims at giving a straightforward account of literature and of writers—straightforward both in content and in language. Critical jargon is as far as possible avoided; any terms that must be used are explained simply; and the constant preoccupation of the authors of the Series is to be lucid.

It is our hope that each book will be easily understood, that it will adequately describe its subject without pretentiousness so that the intelligent reader who wants to know about Donne or Keats or Shakespeare will find enough in it to bring him up to date on critical estimates.

Even those who are well read, we believe, can benefit from a lucid exposition of what they may have taken for granted, and perhaps—dare it be said?—not fully understood.

K. H. G.

E. M. Forster

This book sets out briefly the life and writings of E. M. Forster. His life has been a long one, and his writings, although not prolific, have been diverse. He has already been acclaimed, and he most certainly will be remembered, as a great novelist. While acknowledging his eminence in this field, I have been concerned also to draw attention to the distinction he has brought to his critical and biographical studies, which are penetrating, wide-ranging, and more readily reveal the warmth of the author's personality. On the one hand, he looks back to his family heritage of class and wealth, to evangelical and liberal traditions and, on the other hand, forward to the troubled world of nuclear fission, the exploration of space, and the jeopardy of personal freedom. His is the gift of unerring and uneasy prophecy; but, although there is in his work a vein of deep pessimism, cheerfulness, wit and charm keep bursting in.

Most of his writing explores the relationship between the inner and the outer life, the passion and the prose. Where rapprochement is impossible, he pleads, at least, for tolerance. This present work is aimed at an appraisal of Forster's greatness and at strengthening that plea for tolerance, so that what was excellent in the traditions of western civilisation in the first half of the 20th century will not be lightly swept away in the second half.

I should like to thank Kenneth Grose, the General Editor of the series, for the care and close attention he has given to the manuscript in its various stages of preparation.

M. R.

Contents

Acknowledgements

The author and publishers are indebted to Edmund Nelson and the Provost and Fellows of King's College, Cambridge, for permission to reproduce the cover portrait; to John H. Smith for the photograph of Clouds Hill; to the Press Association for the photograph of the cast of *Howards End*; to Heather Rose for her drawing of Rook's Nest House; and to Charles Mauron for the photograph of E. M. Forster.

They are also indebted to Quentin Bell, Angelica Garnett and The Hogarth Press Ltd., for permission to quote from *Death of a Moth and Other Essays* by Virginia Woolf; to Sidgwick & Jackson Ltd., and the Author's Representatives, for the extracts from *The Study of a Panic* from *The Collected Short Stories* of E. M. Forster; to the author and Edward Arnold (Publishers) Ltd., for the extracts from *Marianne Thornton, Two Cheers for Democracy, Goldsworthy Lowes Dickinson, Abinger Harvest, A Passage to India, The Hill of Devi, Where Angels Fear to Tread, The Longest Journey, A Room with a View* and *Howards End*. The U.S.A. rights are as follows: the excerpts from *Two Cheers for Democracy,* copyright, 1951, by E. M. Forster, and from *A Passage to India* by E. M. Forster, copyright 1924, by Harcourt Brace & World, Inc.; copyright, 1952, by E. M. Forster, are reprinted by permission of Harcourt Brace & World, Inc. The extracts from *Marianne Thornton, Two Cheers for Democracy, Goldsworthy Lowes Dickinson, Abinger Harvest, The Hill of Devi,* and from *Death of a Moth and Other Essays* by Virginia Woolf, are reprinted by permission of Harcourt Brace & World, Inc. The excerpts from *Where Angels Fear to Tread,* by E. M. Forster, copyright 1920 by Alfred A. Knopf, Inc. and renewed 1948 by E. M. Forster, from *The Longest Journey* by E. M. Forster, published 1922 by Alfred A. Knopf, Inc., from *A Room with a View* by E. M. Forster, published 1923 by Alfred A. Knopf, Inc., from *Howards End* by E. M. Forster, published 1921 by Alfred A. Knopf, Inc., and from *The Study of a Panic* from *The Collected Short Stories* of E. M. Forster, published 1947 by Alfred A. Knopf, Inc., are reprinted by permission of the publisher.

The Author

Martial Rose, M.A., L.R.A.M., is Principal of King Alfred's College, Winchester.

Abbreviations

	Title	First published
WA	*Where Angels Fear to Tread*	1905
LJ	*The Longest Journey*	1907
RV	*A Room with a View*	1908
HE	*Howards End*	1910
GE	*The Government of Egypt*	1920
AHG	*Alexandria: A History and a Guide*	1922
PP	*Pharos and Pharillon*	1923
PI	*A Passage to India*	1924
AN	*Aspects of the Novel*	1927
GLD	*Goldsworthy Lowes Dickinson*	1934
AH	*Abinger Harvest*	1936
CSS	*Collected Short Stories*	1947
TC	*Two Cheers for Democracy*	1951
HD	*The Hill of Devi*	1953
MT	*Marianne Thornton*	1956

The editions referred to above are those published by Edward Arnold except AHG (Doubleday & Co.), PP (The Hogarth Press) and CSS (Sidgwick & Jackson).

Rook's Nest House, Stevenage, Hertfordshire—the original Howards End

Clouds Hill—T. E. Lawrence's Dorset cottage, to which Forster was a frequent visitor

E. M. Forster, 1962

E. M. Forster with the cast of the 1967 production of *Howards End*

I

Forster's Life and Work

E. M. Forster was born in 1879. His life very nearly spans a century, from the last government led by Disraeli to the second led by Harold Wilson. At his birth George Eliot was living, Browning and Tennyson, prolific to the end, had many years of work ahead of them. Bernard Shaw had not yet appeared in print, nor had the plays of Ibsen been seen on the English stage. Gladstone was still the vigorous leader of the Liberal Party, and was to come to power several times before the end of the century. It is not Forster's longevity alone that gives him so strong a sense of tradition. He sees in his own family, in his education, and in his liberalism, such ties with the past as need recognising and fortifying if the future of his country and his countrymen is to flourish.

FAMILY

In an essay entitled 'Racial Exercise' Forster traces one branch of his family back to about 1400 in the person of Richard of Sykes Dyke. But as the exercise is to prove how mixed in origin we all are by drawing attention to those branches we cannot trace or those we should prefer uninvestigated, the author's intention is not to call for approbation of the purity of his descent but to stress in 1939

> that we are all of us mongrel, dark haired and light haired, who must learn not to bite one another. TC 29

An element of pride, however, enters into his account of his forebear, Henry Thornton, M.P., the banker who was master of Battersea Rise, a 34-bedroomed house to the west side of Clapham Common. Thornton was a liberal in politics and evangelical in religion. His second cousin and close friend was William Wilberforce. It is with a justifiable pride, without taint of snobbery, that Forster recalls these cousins' struggle to abolish the slave trade. Battersea Rise became the centre of the Clapham Sect with Wilberforce and Thornton at the helm, strongly supported by the Macaulays, Trevelyans, Huxleys and Arnolds. These evangelical reformers accomplished

> the abolition of the slave trade (1807); the emancipation of slaves in the colonies (1833); the founding of the Missionary Society to sponsor Christian teaching in Australia, Africa, and the East (1799); the writing and distributing of edifying tracts for the lower classes; the establishment of *The Christian Observer* (1802), which became a journal of enormous influence; the founding of the British and Foreign Bible Society (1804), the Sunday School Society (1785), the Society for Giving Effect to His Majesty's Proclamation against Vice and Immorality (1799).
>
> Wilfred Stone, THE CAVE AND THE MOUNTAIN, p. 24

Forster is very conscious of this evangelical background and although he winces at the efforts of the palpable do-gooder, so much of his writing, fiction and non-fiction, is directed at achieving some of life's essential freedoms. His freedom from poverty he owes not to his father who died in 1880, but to his godmother, Henry Thornton's daughter, Marianne:

> ... to me she left £8,000. The interest was to be devoted to my education and when I was twenty-five I was to receive the capital. This £8,000 has been the financial salvation of my life. Thanks to it, I was able to go to Cambridge—impossible otherwise, for I failed to win scholarships. After Cambridge I was able to travel for a couple of years, and travelling inclined me to write. After my first visit to India and after the first world war the value of the £8,000 began to diminish, and later on it practically vanished. But by then my writings had begun to sell, and I have been able to live on them instead. Whether—in so stormy an age as ours—this is a reputable sequence I do not know. Still less do I know how the sequence and all sequences will end, with the storms increasing. But I am thankful so far, and thankful to Marianne Thornton; for she and no one else made my career as a writer possible, and her love, in a most tangible sense, followed me beyond the grave.   MT 289

Marianne, his Aunt Monie, died when he was seven. She had oppressed him with presents without finding his heart. In his maturity he expresses his gratitude by writing her biography. He recognises in his great-aunt the grand lady but shies away from her tyranny and the condescension shown to his mother and her family. On the other hand Forster had a deep affection for his maternal grandmother and her family. They were always in a muddle:

> They had no enthusiasm for work, they were devoid of public spirit, and they were averse to piety and quick to detect the falsity sometimes accompanying it . . . it is with her—with them that my heart lies.　　　　　　　　　　　　　　　　　MT 250

Soon after Forster lost his father, his mother moved with her young son to a house in Hertfordshire. Mrs. Forster thought this a safe distance from Aunt Monie's tendency to hunt and corner her. For Forster it was to be an unforgettable background to his boyhood:

> I was brought up as a boy in one of the home counties, in a district which I still think the loveliest in England. There is nothing special about it—it is agricultural land, and could not be described in terms of beauty spots. It must always have looked much the same. I have kept in touch with it, going back to it as to an abiding city and still visiting the house which was once my home, for it is occupied by friends.　　　　　　　　　　　　　　　　　TC 69

The fate that overtook Battersea Rise—it was pulled down to make way for more modern development—struck in Hertfordshire and Forster's familiar and much loved landscape is replaced by a satellite town for 60,000 people. Forster involved himself in two preservation campaigns in Surrey where he and his mother lived from 1903 to 1945. They took the form of pageant plays in which he collaborated with Vaughan Williams who wrote the music. These works protested against the devastation of the countryside in the name of progress.

EDUCATION

Forster was at Tonbridge public school from 1893 to 1897. In *The Longest Journey* he recalls impressions of his schooldays.

'Sawston' with its distinction between day-boys and boarders reflects the author's unpleasant experience at Tonbridge. His subsequent move to Cambridge was like being released from a cage. It brought him freedom, independence and friendship. He was four years at King's College, reading first classics and then history. After Tonbridge he found King's wholly congenial:

> which only admits men who are reading for honours and does not duck an intellectual in the fountain oftener than once in twenty years, apologising elaborately to him afterwards.   GLD 104

Thankful at last to be left alone, to be free to pursue his own interests, Forster found in Cambridge his greatest happiness:

> As Cambridge filled up with friends it acquired a magic quality. Body and spirit, reason and emotion, work and play, architecture and scenery, laughter and seriousness, life and art—these pairs which are elsewhere contrasted were there fused into one. People and books reinforced one another, intelligence joined hands with affection, speculation became a passion, and discussion was made profound by love.   GLD 35

In those early days he numbered among his Cambridge friends John Maynard Keynes, Leonard Woolf, Lytton Strachey, Desmond MacCarthy, Roger Fry, Alfred North Whitehead and Bertrand Russell. Here was the nucleus of the Bloomsbury Group. The Cambridge 'Apostles', as they were called, extended their influence in the larger world. Their liberalism was non-political and in their declaration that facts must yield to ideas they removed themselves rather disdainfully from the hurly-burly of living. Forster never hid in a cultural funk-hole but even his Cambridge friends found him elusive. Leonard Woolf

> nicknamed him the Taupe, partly because of his faint physical resemblance to a mole, but principally because he seemed intellectually and emotionally to travel unseen underground.
> SOWING, AN AUTOBIOGRAPHY OF THE YEARS 1880–1904 p. 171

His first publications (1903–6) in the form of articles and short stories were in a Bloomsbury Group journal, *The Independent Review*.

Among his early short stories are some set in Italy, and Italy was to feature prominently in two of his early novels *Where Angels Fear to Tread* and *A Room With a View*. After graduating in 1901 Forster spent the best part of two years travelling in Italy and Greece. Italy was the land in which repressions were defeated and the restricting conventions of English conduct forgotten. *The Longest Journey*, written between the two Italian novels, *Where Angels Fear to Tread* and *A Room With a View*, is the more poignant because not only does the central character, Rickie, crumble beneath the pressures on him to conform to the acceptable pattern of the English public school master, but also hope for an Italian holiday, a stride towards freedom and happiness, withers.

LIBERALISM

Cambridge and Italy were the major liberating experiences in Forster's life and are clearly reflected in his writing. His two volumes of essays *Abinger Harvest* (1936) and *Two Cheers for Democracy* (1951) containing articles, reviews, poems, broadcast talks, span nearly fifty years. However elusive he was to his Cambridge friends Forster in these works is not timid in declaring where his heart lies. It is manifestly not where Henry Thornton's interests lay: in business; in politics; in great causes. Forster had a healthy respect for money and was fully aware that without his godmother's legacy he would not have enjoyed the leisure for travelling and writing. In politics his inclinations were clearly to the left, but here he was conscious of a collision of loyalties. His writing was made possible through inherited wealth. As a champion of England's beautiful countryside he campaigned against modern housing development, but he knew people must have houses.

> They must, and I think of working-class friends in north London who have to bring up four children in two rooms, and many are even worse off than that.   TC 70

Forster felt, as Lowes Dickinson, that England's scenery trembled 'on the verge of an exquisite mythology'. He himself endeavours to evoke this mythology but, as his work develops, moves beyond England to Italy and India. He was extremely sceptical of the political or social arguments put forward to justify the housing of those in overcrowded slum areas and doubted whether the irreplaceable destruction of a natural beauty that had formed part of a nation's life and tradition could take place without a deep spiritual loss. *Howards End* (1910) on the one hand offers a warmth and security for those who respond to the loveliness of the countryside and on the other predicts the erosion of that beauty by the red rust of creeping London. Hertford, Surrey and even Hampshire are not immune.

Forster springs forward to champion the individual, the sanctity of personal relationships, and, to use Keats's phrase, 'the holiness of the heart's affections' rather than any great cause:

> I hate the idea of causes, and if I had to choose between betraying my country and betraying my friend, I hope I should have the guts to betray my country.   TC 78

From the end of 1915 to the beginning of 1919 Forster was stationed in Alexandria with the International Red Cross. He had cast himself in an inglorious but highly useful role. Three publications owe their origin to this experience: *The Government of Egypt* (1920); *Alexandria: A History and a Guide* (1922); *Pharos and Pharillon* (1923). His patriotism does not lead him to wave flags for the royal family, for our great statesmen, least of all for our colonial empire. He wishes us to cherish and perpetuate the beauty of the countryside, the richness of our culture, and the democracy that protects personal liberty. His liberalism takes a very different form from that of Henry Thornton or William Wilberforce. He not only dislikes causes he distrusts great men:

> They produce a desert of uniformity around them and often a pool of blood too.   TC 82

He would agree with Bertolt Brecht's 'Unhappy the land that needs heroes'. Forster points out that one of the minor merits of democracy is that it does not encourage hero-worship nor produce that unmanageable type of citizen known as the Great

Man. He himself felt more at ease with the humble. When in India in 1921 he was due to meet the Viceroy his reaction was

I can't face important people any more.   HD 88

By contrast Lowes Dickinson on his travels rejoiced at meeting and being regaled by eminent people. He travelled vigorously seeing as much as he could, gleaning what he could of political, religious or philosophical ideas of the countries he visited. Forster's way was to settle in one place and to know well the people with whom he lived and worked. Small wonder that he should write from India

I shine as I could not when Lowes Dickinson and Bob Trevelyan were here.   HD 127

Forster's first two visits to India were in 1912 and 1921. During his second visit he was for six months private secretary to the Maharajah of the State of Dewas Senior in Central India. These visits formed the basis of his last novel *A Passage to India* (1924) and his letters from Dewas published under the title of *The Hill of Devi* (1953). When he returned from his visit to India after the Second World War on the eve of Partition and Independence he had witnessed the extremes of starvation and frustration. He had seen in India an economic failure brought about by the fag-end of Victorian liberalism, which had exploited the backward races abroad and the working classes at home, creating a wake of poverty and hunger—to the point of famine, and gross inequality of opportunity. Yet looking back on his own education, despite the unpleasantness at Tonbridge, Forster thought it humane:

The education I received in those far-off and fantastic days made me soft and I am very glad it did, for I have seen plenty of hardness since, and I know it does not even pay.   TC 67

This education, although it led men to benevolence and philanthropy, to champion freedom of speech and the rights of the individual, did not point to the economic problems ahead. The challenge of that post-war period was to combine the New Economy with the Old Morality. Forster parts company with planning and control systems where personal freedoms are jeopardised. Action taken in the name of the people is meaningless to him:

> I have no mystic faith in the people. I have in the individual.
>
> TC 68

The work of art can help in re-establishing that old morality because it can introduce order into what has been chaos.

> It is valuable because it has to do with order, and creates little worlds of its own, possessing internal harmony, in the bosom of this disordered planet. TC 71

It is the artist, not the Great Man, with whom Forster is at ease. He believes that violence may remain but will never be ultimately triumphant while there is scope for man's creativeness, and for him

> Creation is disinterested. Creation means passionate understanding.
>
> TC 54

'Mr. Andrews' is a strange and unsatisfactory short story yet it states clearly Forster's belief that passionate understanding of man's predicament is a creative act in itself because it extends the frontiers of one personality towards those of another. Mr. Andrews dies and goes to heaven where he and the soul of a dead Turk meet and through mutual unselfishness receive what each had traditionally desired: robes and a harp on the one hand, and numberless virgins on the other. For both their expectations not their hopes are fulfilled. They find heaven dull and so leave.

> As soon as they passed the gate, they felt again the pressure of the world soul. For a moment they stood hand in hand resisting it. Then they suffered it to break upon them, and they, and all the experience they had gained, and all the love and wisdom they had generated, passed into it, and made it better. CSS 186

Victorian liberalism had maintained that society would progress and that conditions of living would improve by man, not abstracting himself from the problem, but by his strenuous effort to alleviate the evils of the world, and the crown of life was to be not a harp but the good effect on other men's lives.

CONCLUSION

Forster's family, education and liberalism are commemorated in his biographies: *Marianne Thornton; Goldsworthy Lowes Dickinson; The Hill of Devi. Marianne Thornton* is a tribute not just to his great-aunt but to his forebears who maintained an admirable tradition of service. Of both his family and his education Forster is proud but not uncritical. His biography of his friend Goldsworthy Lowes Dickinson gives a detailed and glowing account of life in Cambridge at the turn of the century, but Charterhouse for Lowes Dickinson was as gloomy an experience as Tonbridge was for Forster. The invitation to give the Clark lectures at Cambridge in 1927 was a signal honour for one of its most distinguished members. This resulted in *Aspects of the Novel*, a critical work of rare insight.

Cambridge continues to attract Forster, seventy years after he entered its walls as an undergraduate. As an honorary Fellow of King's College, he keeps his rooms and is thought less of a mole than in former days. The timidity of his youth remains in his manner but in his writing he commits himself unflinchingly. *Abinger Harvest, Two Cheers for Democracy*, and *The Hill of Devi* are rich sources of autobiography and testify his aversion to cant, stuffiness and dullness. He frequently poses as the little man, the clown, the anti-hero so that our attention is drawn away from him as an author to observe his more ebullient friends. On one occasion he has his trousers taken from him after an entire chicken fricassée had been spilt over him. He completed this formal luncheon dressed in his host's sky-blue Japanese dressing-gown, with Forster simpering and the guests laughing uproariously throughout. A touch of Charlie Chaplin is felt from time to time.

As an author the most singular fact in his life is that having written five internationally successful novels no further work of fiction has been forthcoming since 1924. There have been biographies, essays, broadcasts, journalism, but no sixth novel.

As Keats had written of poetry so Forster might have considered the craft of fiction:

> Unless it comes not as naturally as the leaves to a tree it had better not come at all.

In this medium he had said what he wished and was sufficiently firm-minded to be silent.

2

Literary Background

Much of Forster's work is a study of personal relationships. He is concerned for the larger world and its modes of government and glad to be living himself in a democracy; but for that democracy he can raise only two cheers. It is

Even love, the beloved Republic, that feeds upon freedom and lives.
A. C. Swinburne, HERTHA

that alone merits three. Forster refers to this line of Swinburne at least three times in his work. He does so, not to conjure up a love that mystically embraces the universe, but to extol a relationship rooted in love, integrity and friendship which can exist between two people. Man is a miracle of creation, whose potential is infinite, but the harmony of two hearts and minds in freedom and in love is sufficient for Forster to raise three cheers.

He himself has most keenly appreciated the society of a small circle of friends. He has been shy and hesitant of meeting the great and powerful, and, despite his prodigious reputation, has a retiring nature. He was as much a fringe member of the Cambridge 'Apostles' as he was of 'the Bloomsbury Group'. His friends found it hard to pin him down. Maynard Keynes described him as 'the elusive colt of a dark horse'. Lytton Strachey at times treated him as a lackey and a porter. Forster's demureness, gentleness and consideration for others were often misinterpreted as a servile anxiety to please, or a failure to know clearly his own mind. As many of his earlier friends condescended to him as a man, so too they carried over this condescension in their criticism of his work. If they were sadly misplaced in their assessment of the man, they were more wildly astray in their evaluation of his work.

Forster, when he examines the work of his contemporaries, shows himself generous, zestful and appreciative. Lowes Dickinson, Lytton Strachey and Virginia Woolf are treated handsomely, despite their own rather disparaging comments on Forster's work. Where he finds his contemporaries tedious or tawdry he refrains from peevish criticism. His reaction to H. G. Wells's science fiction which heralded the glorious Age of the Machine was not a critical diatribe but the short story 'The Machine Stops'. It is indeed a timely warning that the 20th-century machines must not be allowed to break down personal relationships by atrophying human feeling and initiative.

Forster has an ironic temper. He is an acute observer, a just recorder and a disinterested craftsman who will rarely allow an indulgence of personal passions to ruin the pattern of a work of art. In art there must be order, and that order may bring a form and pattern to a world in chaos. The ironic temper senses exquisitely and simultaneously human grandeur and human absurdity. Heavy satire directed at social abuses endeared itself less to Forster than the gentle irony directed at character flaws which cause disharmony in personal relationships. He knew from time to time that he was the butt of others; but he was willing to be so. At Tonbridge there was no escape. At Cambridge, or with his Bloomsbury friends, he could quickly turn into a mole, but a mole that had a shrewd notion of what was happening above ground.

The ironic view of life, as expressed in some aspects of 18th-century literature, particularly commended itself to Forster. Here was to be found the balance of reason and passion, informed classicism, and good taste. Voltaire and Gibbon, for instance, he admired greatly, praising their writing, but not blind to their personal failings. In some ways he makes Voltaire his model:

> If I had to name two people to speak for Europe at the Last Judgment I should choose Shakespeare and Voltaire—Shakespeare for his creative genius, Voltaire for his critical genius and humanity.

> Voltaire cared for truth, he believed in tolerance, he pitied the oppressed, and since he was a forceful character he was able to drive his ideas home. They happen to be my own ideas, and like many other small people I am thankful when a great person comes along and says for me what I can't say properly for myself.   TC 174

Voltaire was anti-Nazi in the time of Frederick the Great. His call for liberation from the forces of tyranny was on both personal and national grounds, and his spirit of cultivated defiance informed so many of Forster's broadcasts during the Second World War, in which he dealt not with the larger political issues but with personal values, which might yet be cherished if our freedom from tyranny were secured.

The romantic poets, in particular Wordsworth, Shelley and Byron, had uttered loud and penetrating cries for freedom. At the beginning of the 20th century Wordsworth was often considered more naïve than sublime, and Byron, as a champion of nationalism, somewhat suspect, when sabres were rattled in Prussian scabbards. But to a group of Cambridge intellectuals at the turn of the century Shelley's poetry proclaimed freedom, intellectual and spiritual, shaking off the old shackles imposed by the old gods, and the unseating of those tyrannical deities. Shelley was calling them to realise a personal fulfilment that conventional living would have denied them. A great deal of the 'Apostles' creed was contained in 'Prometheus Unbound'.

> Gentleness, Virtue, Wisdom, and Endurance,
> These are the seals of that most firm assurance
> Which bars the pit over Destruction's strength.

Shelley's image of the Titan, Prometheus, the fire-bringer and friend of man, breaking away from the age-old tyranny of Zeus, burned in the minds of those idealistic young men who were turning their thoughts from the 19th to the 20th century.

> To suffer woes which Hope thinks infinite;
> To forgive wrongs darker than death or night;
>   To defy Power, which seems omnipotent;
> To love, and bear; to hope till Hope creates

From its own wreck the thing it contemplates;
  Neither to change, nor falter, nor repent;
This, like thy glory, Titan, is to be
Good, great and joyous, beautiful and free;
This is alone Life, Joy, Empire, and Victory.

Brave words for the aspirant Edwardians who responded to Shelley's Greek-like demand for beauty and freedom. His 'Epipsychidion', commemorating an Italian lady, Emilia, trapped in a convent as a bird in a cage, is constantly in Forster's mind as he writes *The Longest Journey*. Above all, Shelley's scorn of the restricting influence of the conventions of English society, matched by his delight in the warmth and liberality of his reception in Italy, captured the sympathy of those young travellers who had capitulated to the magic of Florence, Bologna or Ravello.

The heroics that Shelley inspired in a small group of intellectuals at the turn of the 19th century were not those familiar to the Victorian age. None leapt to extend the frontiers of the Empire. Great causes, heroes and hero-worship, were suspect. Forster and his fellow-thinkers were advocating independence of thought and freedom of action based on personal rather than national attitudes and beliefs.

The decline of the hero in literature dates from this time. Forster's heroes themselves, Rickie and Philip for instance, have a way of fainting at the most critical moments. The central character of Hardy's novel *Jude the Obscure* (1896) is defeated in all his endeavours: as a scholar, stonemason, lover, husband, father. His attempt to gain an education, from which his humble birth precludes him, is thwarted by his own weakness of character, by the play of circumstances, and by the rigid thinking of the times. The Victorian era, the age of heroes, draws to a close with one of its finest works depicting failure. Jude is crushed by the time he lives in. This novel was greeted with an outburst of vitriolic abuse, almost as intense as that directed against the first performances of Ibsen's plays in this country. It was called 'Jude the Obscene' and denounced from the pulpit. After its publication Hardy lived for more than thirty years but wrote no more novels.

Jude made way for the anti-hero in modern literature. He was defeated by more than his own failings. The society in which he lived and died is indicted by Hardy for its injustice, hypocrisy, illiberality and lack of compassion. The age that saw the beginning of compulsory education, the working men's clubs, the evening institutes, saw also the many hopes of learning and advancement dashed by a class structure and social code that sought to maintain the old hierarchies. In America examples abounded of men rapidly acquiring massive fortunes: in England the poor man, the little man, was excessively restricted by class conventions. The earliest films of Charlie Chaplin depicted the predicament of the little man in a large, unfriendly, industrial society. There is in him a yearning for heroism and love but, alas, he is not Prince Hamlet. He lacks nobility of birth, a high tragic theme, and grandeur in death. The films and literature of 'the little men' have continued to satisfy a general 20th-century need for such fantasy, and the experiences in Europe of the 1914–18 years reinforced this need.

Among the authors whose work meant most to Forster during the First World War were Blake, William Morris and T. S. Eliot.

> The people I really clung to were those who had nothing tangible to offer.... They took me into a country where the will is not everything, and the braying patriots of the moment made no sound.
>
> AH 73

T. S. Eliot's early poems reflected the uncertainty and bewilderment of the age.

> No! I am not Prince Hamlet, nor was meant to be; ...
> At times, indeed, almost ridiculous—
> Almost, at times, the Fool. ...
> Shall I part my hair behind? Do I dare to eat a peach?
> I shall wear white flannel trousers, and walk upon the beach.
> I have heard the mermaids singing each to each.
> I do not think that they will sing to me.

Forster recoiled from the religious certainties of T. S. Eliot's later verse and rejected with some considerable distaste the account of Celia's martyrdom in *The Cocktail Party*. He did not

23

take kindly to the doctrine of atonement nor show any enthusiasm for a creed which made a virtue of pain and suffering. The death-bed scenes, so cherished by the Victorian readers of Dickens and George Eliot for their moral uplift and religious fervour, are deliberately avoided by both Jane Austen and Forster, to whom dwelling on pain and death is tantamount to bad taste. Their attitude is not myopic, merely selective. Passions, too deeply moved, blur judgment, and both writers value and respect clear judgment in their readers. Without judgment the order and beauty of a work of art may not be perceived. The age of heroes may have passed but the love of beauty remains, and it was in the poet and the artist that Shelley's 20th-century disciples saw 'the unacknowledged legislators of the world'.

> The work of art stands up by itself, and nothing else does. It achieves something which has often been promised by society, but always delusively. Ancient Athens made a mess—but the 'Antigone' stands up. Renaissance Rome made a mess—but the ceiling of the Sistine got painted. James I made a mess—but there was 'Macbeth'. Louis XIV—but there was 'Phèdre'. Art for art's sake? I should just think so, and more so than ever at the present time (1949). It is the one orderly product which our muddling race has produced.
> TC 101

Much 19th-century literature is characterised by a spirit of optimism, heroism and romance. Good and bad were clearly distinguishable. At the end of novels and plays the good prospered, the evil suffered. Affectation was ridiculed, hypocrisy exposed. The *Antigone* and *Macbeth* stand up because as works of art they generate their own life and order, and when tested against our understanding, on the one hand, of the conflict of the rights of the individual with the rights of the state and, on the other, of the nature of ambition, we must say 'Yes, this is true'. These works are not contained within the age in which they were written by their author's compliance with social and moral codes then in existence. Dickens will entertain us vastly without our ever responding with 'Yes, this is true'. The essential difference between, say, Trollope and Conrad, between *Barchester*

Towers and *The Heart of Darkness* is that the former may remain an amusing and informative comment on ecclesiastical life in a cathedral city in the middle of the 19th century, while the latter drives at a universal truth about the nature of man.

Forster's work drives at a universal truth about the nature of man but not in Conrad's path of hopeless heroism, tragedy and pessimism. There are no heroic characters in his novels; his central characters can muster between them few heroic qualities. Ibsen and Chekhov too present us with scarcely one wholly admirable character, yet the overall impression is of beauty in life and grandeur in man:

> The characters may no longer be heroes sublime even in their fall, they may be the ordinary men and women of Ibsen and Chekhov, over whose lack of tragic splendour critics have mourned so needlessly. Complaining of the want of great personalities in this play or that, they forget the author. For the characters may be poor in spirit and feeble in desire, and the play remain tragic in spite of it, if we feel that the author is himself none of these things and has never cheated or paltered in his picture of men as they are.
>
> F. L. Lucas, TRAGEDY

'As a rule', wrote Forster, 'if a writer has a romantic temperament, he will find human relationships beautiful.' It was on the subject of personal relationships that Forster and some of his literary friends showed both a romantic temperament and a measure of optimism, but the larger world of politics, power and industrialisation was seen as squalid and ugly. T. E. Lawrence, for instance, may have been driven to his desert heroics through a revulsion from the 20th-century civilisation. He loved the half-savage Arabs because they challenged that civilisation. His subsequent role as Private Shaw was an anti-heroic gesture which came as no surprise to Forster who on reading *The Seven Pillars of Wisdom* (1926) had detected

> beneath the gallant fighting and the brilliant description of scenery— sensitiveness, introspection, doubt, disgust at the material world.
>
> TC 287

Conrad, Joyce and D. H. Lawrence were the most distinguished writers who had no link with the Bloomsbury Group. Conrad died in 1924, the year in which *Passage to India* was published. He lived quietly in the country and was at pains to keep himself apart from the literary bustle of the day. The theme of moral isolation is repeated in his works and his own personal seclusion may well have supported such a theme. So many of his central characters are alone and lost in the tempest of life and have to find themselves in the battle against the elements. Conrad cherishes the heroic impulses in man but frequently shows us, without cynicism, the ashes that result. Both Conrad and T. E. Lawrence stretch their canvas wide—beyond personal relationships. There are journeys to be taken, pilgrimages to be made. Ultimately, it is the elements, sea and sand, that sift man.

Joyce's *Ulysses* (1922) is a pilgrimage of a very different kind. It is a journey into the mind and shows the deep influence of the insight into human motivation provided by the work of Sigmund Freud. Joyce's extreme experiments in style and treatment struck Forster at first as an aberration of art but he recognised Joyce's genius and particularly welcomed the close psychological probing into the nature of man:

> Man is beginning to understand himself better and to explore his own contradictions. . . . It has brought a great enrichment to the art of fiction. It has given subtleties and depths to the portrayal of human nature. The presence in all of us of the subconscious, the occasional existence of the split personality, the persistence of the irrational especially in people who pride themselves on their reasonableness, the importance of dreams and the prevalence of day-dreaming—here are some of the points which novelists have seized on and which have not been ignored by historians. This psychology is not new, but it has newly risen to the surface.   TC 282

D. H. Lawrence, who with a crusading spirit was forever stirring to revolt the Calibans of the subconscious, was fiercely critical of Forster's Cambridge and Bloomsbury friends. He had spurned the overtures of friendship made him by Keynes and Bertrand Russell. He showed both jealousy and contempt and would have no truck with them because they lacked reverence. Both Forster and Lawrence are critical of cerebration, aesthetics, art as a shield against life. Forster's Stephen Wonham (*The*

Longest Journey) in his physical response to life and uncluttered mind, is in some measure analogous to some of D. H. Lawrence's heroes; but in Forster's work obedience to the blood-beat results in a richer and more complex fulfilment than the gratification of sexual desire. Forster revered Lawrence as a prophet but rejected him as a preacher and this valid distinction is made in *Aspects of the Novel*. He had described Lawrence as the greatest imaginative novelist of his generation and when he spoke in court at 'The Trial of Lady Chatterley' (1961) he was pleased to reaffirm the highest regard he had for Lawrence.

Undoubtedly the Bloomsbury Group, containing a most gifted set of writers and artists, exerted the greatest influence on English literary affairs in the first part of this century. At the centre of the group were Leonard and Virginia Woolf, Vanessa and Clive Bell, Duncan Grant, Lytton Strachey, Roger Fry, Goldsworthy Lowes Dickinson and Maynard Keynes. On the periphery, similar to the fringe position he had held with the 'Apostles', was Forster. Collectively his friends were a high-powered group of intellectuals of middle and upper-middle class families, enjoying the inherited wealth of sound investments. Individually they were hardworking deep-thinking progressives, concerned to preserve what was best of the past and to forge new art forms for the future. It could be said of Keynes that his brilliance in economics and the innovations he initiated corresponded to the creative achievement of his Bloomsbury friends. Unlike Dickinson and Keynes the majority of the group retreated from the field of politics into the field of art. It was a withdrawal from what seemed squalid, self-seeking, destructive and ugly, into a world where beauty could still be championed and personal relationships revered. They naturally came under fire for their parasitic smugness. Their aristocracy of thought shut them off from a range of experience which might have deepened their creative work.

The group launched both the *Independent Review*, in whose early editions some of Forster's short stories were published, and also the Hogarth Press. They were concerned as much with the presentation of literature as with the literature itself. William

Morris had set them principles of publishing they were proud to follow. They were entirely sympathetic with Morris's protest against the ugliness of commerce and industry. Although far from a guilt-laden society, the most prominent members of the group were fascinated by the attention to motivation now made possible by recent research in psychology. In Virginia Woolf's 'Waves', for instance, not only do poetic and prose forms merge, but so also do the conscious and subconscious states. Prose was upheld as the precious link between one civilisation and another. The Bloomsbury Group supported George Orwell on this vital issue:

> He was passionate over the purity of prose, . . . he tears to bits some passages of contemporary writing. It is a dangerous game—the contemporaries can always retort—but it ought to be played, for if prose decays, thought decays and all the finer roads of communication are broken. Liberty, he argues, is connected with prose, and bureaucrats who want to destroy liberty tend to write and speak badly, and to use pompous or woolly or portmanteau phrases in which their true meaning or any meaning disappears.　　　TC74

Interest in the psychology of the subconscious, which has bedevilled the prose of the bureaucrats, the power-seekers, the pseudo-scientists, added clarity and vision to the work of Lytton Strachey. The treatment of both his Queens, Elizabeth and Victoria, is marked by his imaginative insight into their childhood days. In the case of Victoria, as death takes hold of her she recalls her younger days. Lytton Strachey was delighted to receive from Freud, to whom he had sent a complimentary copy of *Elizabeth and Essex*, warm appreciation of his work:

> As a historian, then, you show that you are steeped in the spirit of psycho-analysis. And . . . you have approached one of the most remarkable figures in your country's history, you have known how to trace back her character to the impressions of her childhood, you have touched upon her most hidden motives with equal boldness and discretion, and it is very possible that you have succeeded in making a correct reconstruction of what actually occurred.
>
> Michael Holroyd, LYTTON STRACHEY, p. 616

Forster has shown that he favours a fringe position. It is as evident in his relationship with his Cambridge and Bloomsbury friends as in his welcome of psychology, or the anti-hero in literature. He is not one to be swept away by movements in art or literature, but throughout he has maintained a vigorous independence. He was as Virginia Woolf perceived

> extremely susceptible to the influence of the time

without losing his belief that it was the private life in which was to be found the soul's eternity.

3

Fiction I

Forster's short stories were all written before 1914; that is, between 1901, the year of his leaving Cambridge, and at least nine years before the publication of his last novel *Passage to India*. In his introduction to the collected edition, first published in 1948, he calls them fantasies. It is a mode which he later glances at but to which he is never again to return. The time is out of joint, he explains, for such a return. The leisured world of the *fin de siècle*, the spaciousness of the Edwardian era, through which Fantasy might flit 'over scenes of Italian and English holidays' or might wing her way towards countries of the future, has contracted and has been fretted with new frontiers. Fantasy might well break free from the fetters of upper middle-class stuffiness, might well be invoked to summon up Pan, the primal spirit of the wood, or Hermes, the messenger of the gods, the machine breaker, but in an age when Pan and Hermes are less exceptional, more credible, and more unreined, fantasy must find other forms.

Coleridge's account of his composing 'Kubla Khan' was rooted in Forster's mind, and he found in the story of the man from Porlock an example of inspirational writing analogous to his own experience of writing 'The Story of a Panic'. Coleridge, when staying at a lonely farmhouse near the Somerset–Devon border and under the influence of laudanum, fell asleep and had a most powerful and vivid dream. On waking he feverishly set about writing out the poem that had been given him in the vision, but was stopped by a stranger from Porlock entering the cottage and preventing the completion of the work, for on the intruder's departure the poet's inspiration had left him.

Forster tells us how, although conscious and without the aid of drugs, inspiration came to him:

> ... the attendant circumstances remain with me vividly. After I came down from Cambridge—the Cambridge to which I have just returned—I travelled abroad for a year, and I think it was in the May of 1902 that I took a walk near Ravello. I sat down in a valley, a few miles above the town, and suddenly the first chapter of the story rushed into my mind as if it had waited for me there. I received it as an entity and wrote it out as soon as I returned to the hotel. But it seemed unfinished and a few days later I added some more until it was three times as long; as now printed. Of these two processes, the first—that of sitting down on the theme as if it were an anthill—has been rare. I did it again next year in Greece, where the whole of 'The Road from Colonus' hung ready for me in a hollow tree not far from Olympia.   V. CSS

This mode of inspirational writing Forster might think the purest but it is, he knows, not infallible; and he instances the story that did not succeed. Short stories and poems, more easily than novels, might result from such momentary bursts of creative activity. The longer art form calls for more strenuous and extended intellectual effort, for patience and planning, for a notion of grand design. The inspiration which might sustain 'The Story of a Panic' would flag sadly for such a work as *Howards End*.

`The man from Porlock, the dream-breaker, features repeatedly in the short stories. His tiresome banalities characterise the British abroad, in Italy and Greece, his cringing to the Establishment is characterised in Feo in 'The Eternal Moment' or Inskip, the tutor, in 'Other Kingdom'. The dream-breaker is there to give credibility to the dream. Although Forster himself wrote only two of the stories in consequence of an inspirational flash, most of the tales in contrasting the real world with the fantasy world stress the physical and spiritual restrictions of the one compared with the freedom and joy of the other. The visionary or dreamer may have more important things to say about the reality of life than the so-called realist, who scoffs at fantasy partly out of ignorance partly out of fear; that is fear of acknowledging the forces of nature, and ignorance of the powers of imagination.

'*The Story of a Panic*'

Place and story are often strongly linked if not inseparables in Forster's work, and one might guess that when the author in May 1902 sat down in a valley, a few miles above the town of Ravello, it was to look on a scene such as is described as the venue of the picnic:

> The valley ended in a vast hollow, shaped like a cup, into which radiated ravines from the precipitous hills around. Both the valley and the ravines and the ribs of hill that divided the ravines were covered with leafy chestnut, so that the general appearance was that of a many-fingered green hand, palm upwards, which was clutching convulsively to keep us in its grasp. Far down the valley we could see Ravello and the sea, but that was the only sign of another world.
> CSS 3

The natural landscape is in itself compelling in a magical sense, so that men's actions are not wholly consciously directed. Something of this magic lingers in the dell at Madingley where in *The Longest Journey* Rickie and Agnes embrace, and also in the clearing in *A Room With a View* which is the scene of a moment of passion between Lucy and George Emerson.

The great god Pan can speak directly to the young, the country-rooted, the unsophisticated. His music may screech discordantly but its call is for freedom. Niceness, social decorum, priggishness, aesthetic appraisal, are ill-matched against the cats-paw of a wind that sends sophistication scampering and stirs in man animalistic fears and joys. On Italian soil and in the Italian character or even in the unspoilt responsive English, Forster implies, Pan's power is often manifest.

Eustace, a fourteen-year-old boy, is one of a small group of English staying in Ravello who go on a picnic. His compatriots condescend to the Italians whom they find crude, mercenary and socially inferior. They condescend even to the landscape.

Those sweet chestnuts of the South are puny striplings compared
with our robust Northerners.   CSS 5

The picnickers finish their lunch and in the ensuing conversation smugly conclude in the re-echoing words 'The great God
Pan is dead'. During this conversation Eustace has been carving
a whistle from a piece of tree trunk. Now he blows it. The
noise is excruciating, ear-splitting and discordant. But it sum-
mons Pan. He is felt as a wisp of wind. The English, filled with
blind terror, stampede through the undergrowth, over the rocks
and down to the valley below. Eustace alone stays where he is.
When his friends return they find him smiling strangely. He has
apparently experienced nothing of the bestial terror which
clutched at their hearts. He has been joyously possessed. A goat's
footmarks are seen in the moist earth beneath the trees.

Eustace's experience of Pan remains a mystery, locked from
the adults, but vaguely apprehended by Rose, a young lady in
the party, and wholly grasped by the intuitive young Italian
servant, Gennaro, whom Eustace meets on his return to the hotel.
Capering, whooping and leaping, Eustace has hurried back to
Ravello. He calls for Gennaro and leaps into his arms when he
sees him. Gennaro is not surprised. 'Ho capito', he says. 'I understand.' The distinction is underlined between the directness and
affection of animal spirits and stiffened reserve of well-bred
conformity. The story-teller deplores the lack of decorum:

> I always make a point of behaving pleasantly to Italians, however
> little they may deserve it; but this habit of promiscuous intimacy
> was perfectly intolerable, and could only lead to familiarity and
> mortification for all. Taking Miss Robinson [Eustace's aunt] aside, I
> asked her permission to speak seriously to Eustace on the subject
> of intercourse with social inferiors. She granted it; but I determined
> to wait till the absurd boy had calmed down a little from the
> excitement of the day. Meanwhile, Gennaro, instead of attending to
> the wants of the two ladies, carried Eustace into the house, as if it
> was the most natural thing in the world.   CSS 16

During the night it is discovered that Eustace has left his
bedroom and is running about outside, now singing, now

chattering wildly. The well-meaning English chase him, trap him, bundle him back to his room, and lock him in it. Gennaro, generously bribed, has helped in the capture but acknowledges his betrayal:

> 'He longed for a friend, and found none for fifteen years. Then he found me, and the first night I—I who have been in the woods and understood things too—betray him to you and send him in to die.'
>
> CSS 27

But Eustace does not die. When Gennaro had been possessed by Pan he survived because as he says,

> '... I have neither parents nor relatives nor friends, so that, when the first night came, I could run through the woods, and climb the rocks, and plunge into the water, until I had accomplished my desire.'

Gennaro then frees Eustace from the imprisonment imposed on him by his relatives and friends and leaps with him in his arms from the first story on to the asphalt path. Eustace jumps over the parapet of the garden wall and disappears shouting and laughing into the valley. The leap that frees Eustace, however, kills Gennaro.

In 'The Story of a Panic' age opposes youth, sophistication is set against natural forces, reasoned action against impulse, the tame against the wild. When powerful and magical forces haunt certain places it is as well to be at harmony with the *genius loci*. Both the wooded valley near Ravello and the Malabar Caves of *A Passage to India* are places in which a *genius loci* exerts great influence on the actions of men. Such primeval forces we may not understand: we should do well therefore to acknowledge their existence and to respect them.

The short stories are too many to be dealt with separately within the space of this chapter. Indeed, some though short are tedious; in some the humour is feeble and in others the style gauche. Yet common themes emerge, some of which find no echoes in later work, while others prove themselves capable of full development by the mature novelist.

Pan's power is felt not only in 'The Story of a Panic' but also in 'Other Kingdom', 'The Curate's Friend' and 'The Story of the Siren'. In these stories the forces of conventional respectability are bewildered and frightened by the fey. Nature which has hitherto been distanced, so that it can be made the subject of a poem or a painting, so that it can be admired aesthetically or tamed territorially with bridges, paths and hedges, suddenly scorns such controls and unleashes a power beyond the comprehension of the civilised, tidy-minded community.

In 'Other Kingdom' it is Miss Beaumont whom Pan claims for his own. Harcourt Worters, a wealthy Hertfordshire landowner,

> had picked her out of Ireland and brought her home, without money, without connections, almost without antecedents, to be his bride.   CSS 68

His intention is to shape her by the accepted methods of the upper middle-class English educational system into the wife he would wish. He gives her a tutor to cultivate her mind and a beech wood for her recreational pleasure. Latin and Greek would discipline her mind, and he, Harcourt, would show her how her copse could be improved by introducing a bridge, a fence, a gate with two keys, and an asphalt path. Miss Beaumont's zest for her studies, her gay affinity to her fellow-student, Ford, and her impulsive behaviour, compel Mr. Worters to circumscribe her actions and she complains

> 'He won't let me do what I want. Latin and Greek began it; I wanted to know about gods and heroes and he wouldn't let me: then I wanted no fence round Other Kingdom and no bridge and no path—and look.'   CSS 82

But Pan-possessed spirits will not be thus flouted. They will be neither tamed nor 'civilised'. Miss Beaumont escapes from Worters because she is choked by his wish to dominate her, to restrict her freedom, to distort *her* Other Kingdom into his. She has not, as Worters at first suspects, eloped with Ford, but she apparently abandons human form to assume a wood spirit's existence. Such a notion is beyond Worters:

> 'I found her no better than a savage, I trained her, I educated her. But I'll break them both. I can do that; I'll break them soul and body.'   CSS 88

But it is not beyond Ford:

> 'She has escaped you absolutely, for ever and ever, as long as there are branches to shade men from the sun.'   CSS 89

Place

'The place has nothing to do with it at all', exclaims Mrs. Herriton (*Where Angels Fear to Tread*) when she hears that her widowed daughter-in-law, travelling in Italy, has become engaged to be married. She is wrong. Place has everything to do with it, and in Forster's work there is an acute sensitivity to place. The *genius loci* is as powerful and pervasive in the short stories as in the early novels or in *Howards End* or *Passage to India*. The Faun inhabits the beech copse of 'The Curate's Friend' as the mermaid holds sway within the waters of the grotto in 'The Story of the Siren'. And even in those short stories without fauns, nymphs, dryads or sylphs 'place' is of paramount significance.

Place has seemingly no significance in the restructured automated world of the Machine. In 'The Machine Stops' Pekin and Shrewsbury are indistinguishable. It is against the blurring of spatial identity that Kuno reacts. His mother, a true daughter of the Machine, when flying over the Roof of the World said,

> 'Cover the window please. Those mountains give me no ideas.'
>   CSS 140

Kuno, aware that the Machine has robbed man of the sense of space and touch and reduced every human relation, ventures out of the Machine at the risk of his life to see the hills of Wessex as 'Aelfrid saw them when he overthrew the Danes'.

In 'The Road to Colonus' Mr. Lucas's sense of fulfilling his destiny by developing a relationship with a particular place is as strong as Kuno's. But whereas Kuno is young, impulsive, persistent, Mr. Lucas is old and weak, and his moment of vision of a kingdom to be regained is fleeting:

> To sleep in the Khan with the gracious, kind-eyed country people . . . one such night would place him beyond relapse . . .

His wishes are pooh-poohed by his strong-willed daughter and her brisk companions and he is forcibly moved on. Later, on his return to England, he is told of a disaster that overtook this particular Greek Khan. The information to him is inconsequential. He has missed his moment of affirmation, the vision has faded, and he has relapsed without any vestige of greatness into a petulant, complaining dotage.

Place of birth, place of growth, place of death, matter deeply. When they cease to matter deeply, as in the Machine age, an essential part of man has died. Place matters to Harcourt Worters; but only so that he might own it, control it, and distort its natural form, and Forster directs against Worters the lash of irony that he later lets fall on another 'spoiler', Henry Wilcox (*Howards End*), who seems equally insensitive to the sanctity of place.

First Hand, Second Hand

The traditionalist accepts inherited mores and standards, accepts class patterns of behaviour and aesthetic criteria. Colonel Leyland ('The Eternal Moment') is as traditional in the old world as Vashti ('The Machine Stops') is in the new. It is the young, the artists and the poets who see visions, who challenge accepted values, and will have no truck with the second hand. The short stories repeatedly align the old-hat second-raters against those who would perish rather than compromise their vision. Mr. Lucas ('The Road from Colonus') compromised and the moment of relevation was not even remembered. Miss Raby ('The Eternal Moment') still cherishes a moment of love twenty years after the event and returns to recapture it. Place and persons have changed, but she still must put her question:

> 'Answer "yes" or "no"; that day when you said you were in love with me—was it true?'   CSS 244

But she is no longer speaking to an impulsive young guide, but to a seasoned concierge with his eye on the main chance. He is incapable of a first-hand response, and it is ironic that his corruption has been occasioned by the popularisation of his home village by Miss Raby's novel 'The Eternal Moment'. He is an Italian-speaking German who earns his living by fleecing the English visitors to Vorta. In twenty years his village has changed, and with it his personality. In so many of Forster's short stories the Italian, like the child, speaks from the heart and speaks true. In this concierge, Feo, the virtue of his nationality has been eroded, and Miss Raby's breathtaking forthrightness elicits from him as much embarrassment as it does from Colonel Leyland.

> She looked at the dishevelled Feo, fat, perspiring, and unattractive, and smiled sadly at her own stupidity, not at his. It was useless to speak to him again; her talk had scared away his competence and his civility, and scarcely anything was left. He was hardly more human than a frightened rabbit. 'Poor man', she murmured, 'I have only vexed him. . . . I wish he would have answered my question, if only out of pity. He does not know the sort of thing that keeps me alive.'   CSS 244

Age and material considerations have transformed Feo from the passionate young man who declared his love for Miss Raby, but she has kept her vision of that moment and has to suffer the harsh realisation that in lesser spirits second-hand soon supersedes first-hand experience. The young can see clearly, feel sharply, know intuitively: Gennaro and Rose ('The Story of a Panic') sense Eustace's predicament as Ford ('Other Kingdom') understands Miss Beaumont's; the boy in 'The Celestial Omnibus' is at ease in the exalted company in which he finds himself whereas Mr. Bons, the president of the Literary Society, goes to pieces. He could manage Dante and Chaucer in book form but not face to face. In 'The Machine Stops' Vashti has complacently surrendered her individuality to the Machine to the point where first-hand experience is painful to her. She is horrified at the prospect of the sun striking her face and is relieved when the Himalayas are hidden behind the metal blind of the airship. When the airship attendant puts out her hand to stop her falling

Vashti is filled with revulsion. In the Age of the Machine people never touch one another. Kuno, her son, on the other hand struggles to free himself from the Machine. He wants to tread on the surface of the earth, to see the stars, and make physical contact with other human beings. He will not accept the Machine's propaganda:

> 'Beware of first-hand ideas.' '. . . First-hand ideas do not really exist. They are but the physical impressions produced by love and fear, and on this gross foundation who could erect a philosophy? Let your ideas be second-hand, and if possible tenth-hand, for then they will be far removed from that disturbing element—direct observation.' CSS 145

Vashti, however, who has rejected direct observation, readily adjusts herself to the increasing defects of the Machine when it begins to disintegrate. The ultimate breakdown inevitably brings disaster to those bereft of individuality and initiative.

Summary

The short stories on the whole are light entertainment thinly veiling an impassioned plea that we should observe more closely the roots from which we spring, giving rein to the life of the senses and the life of the imagination. At the beginning of the 20th century Forster saw quite clearly the threat offered by rapid industrialisation to the English countryside and to our individuality. He feared that the Machine might control us and turn us into a drab uniformity, all living in identical boxes, eating the same food, hearing the same sounds, seeing the same sights, thinking the same thoughts. The short stories reaffirm Forster's belief that there is a mystery in life not subject to rational analysis, and that the wonder of the world might best be apprehended by those who young in spirit and independent in mind draw their strength and joy from the earth that made them and will eventually receive them.

'WHERE ANGELS FEAR TO TREAD'

Forster's first novel begins and ends with a rail journey: the first from England to Italy; the second from Italy to England. In between there are two deaths, Lilia and her baby; and two of the central figures, Philip Herriton and Caroline Abbott, undergo experiences which radically affect their characters. In essence this seems the pattern for a tragedy, but for most of the book the author's treatment of his theme is light, gay and even comic. In tone the penultimate chapter is entirely in contrast. It is passionate, tense and violent. The final chapter, which indicates the extent of the character development, has to resolve the preceding violence and yet return us to England not too greatly bruised. There is consequently a structural imbalance in the novel which may reflect the author's reluctance to give themes of pain and death sufficient weight to achieve an integrated novel. At the beginning of the last chapter of *Mansfield Park* Jane Austen had written:

> Let other pens dwell on guilt and misery. I quit such odious subjects as soon as I can, impatient to restore everybody, not greatly in fault themselves, to tolerable comfort, and to have done with all the rest.

Forster, too, has no wish to dwell on guilt and misery, but neither will he ignore them. But the transition from the scene in which Gino tortures Philip to that in which we are prepared to return to the relative calm of England suburban life with its garden parties and prayer meetings, is uneasy. However, *Where Angels Fear to Tread* as a first novel remains a *tour de force*. It is magnificently written and contains certain passages as memorable as anything from his maturer work. More remarkable, it is not the work of an apprentice but a master craftsman.

The axis of the novel has its poles in England and Italy: Sawston and Monteriano. Sawston is to feature in *The Longest Journey* but there it is identified with the public school (Tonbridge) rather than the small country town. In the Sawston of *Where Angels Fear to Tread* Mrs. Herriton holds pride of place. She is genteel, moneyed, proud, domineering and unimaginative. The place she lives in takes on these characteristics. Monteriano is old and has locked in it the mystery and wisdom of age. It has its beauty too, not only the paintings in Santa Deodata's, but also its buildings, its views and its age. Lilia's visit to Italy is an escape from Sawston and what it stands for: 'its petty unselfishness', its 'mediocrity and dullness, and spitefulness and society'. She wished in particular to escape from Mrs. Herriton in whom 'pride was the only solid element. She could not bear to seem less charitable than others'. Monteriano and Gino charm her simultaneously. She sees him one evening

> . . . sitting on the mud wall that faced the Volterra gate. She remembered how the evening sun had struck his hair, and how he had smiled down at her, and being both sentimental and unrefined, was determined to have the man and the place together.   WA 48

She marries Gino and they live in the house facing the Volterra gate. She soon discovers there is primitivism as well as beauty in man and place.

In his way Philip strives as much as Lilia to escape Sawston and its influence. His mother dominates and frightens him, but he sees clearly that her life is without meaning:

> To what purpose was her diplomacy, her insincerity, her continued repression of vigour?   WA 98

Lilia was crushed by her. For Irma, Lilia's daughter, she is more concerned to correct her grammar than show affection. Mrs. Theobald, Lilia's mother, is beneath her contempt. Mrs. Herriton is the first lady of Sawston, and Sawston, Forster would have us believe, is a typical English country town at the beginning of the century. It abounds in bigotry, hypocrisy and ugliness. Has Italy anything better to offer? Something very different at least.

As Philip gives Lilia last minute advice on Charing Cross station before she leaves for Italy he says

> 'And, don't, let me beg you, go with that awful tourist idea that Italy's only a museum of antiquities and art. Love and understand the Italians, for the people are more marvellous than the land.'
>
> WA7

Lilia in part takes his advice. She loves an Italian without understanding him or his race. Philip has cause to rue his advice when he watches Lilia's husband eating spaghetti 'when those slippery worms were flying down his throat' because he finds he is not sitting opposite a gentleman. It would seem that the Englishman either condescends to the Italian as Philip does, or, as Lilia, sentimentalises him. It is only when Philip and Caroline begin to understand the Italian, that they themselves are changed. Italy not Sawston has the transmuting power. It does not ultimately change Harriet although momentarily it makes of that pillar of Sawston's society both a kidnapper and a killer.

Characterisation

Harriet becomes the kidnapper and consequently primarily responsible for the baby's death because of a surprising change in her character. Hitherto we have recognised Harriet as a 'flat' character as defined by Forster in *Aspects of the Novel*. She is practically a type or a caricature. Her reaction in any situation is predictable. She will show concern for her inlaid box which she had lent to Lilia, defend stoutly the most treasured institutions of provincial England—the Church, the Book Club, the Debating Society, the Progressive Whist, the bazaars, and on railway journeys be much troubled by smuts in the eye. As Philip says, she had 'bolted all the cardinal virtues and couldn't digest them'.

Mrs. Herriton's instructions to Harriet are to accompany Philip to Monteriano and to ensure that he is successful in returning with the baby. At the moment when Harriet believes Philip will be unsuccessful she

> had gone prepared for an interview with Gino, and finding him out, she had yielded to a grotesque temptation.

This action and Harriet's consequent furtiveness turn her from a 'flat' into a 'round' character. Flat characters are very useful to an author

> since they never need reintroducing, never run away, have not to be watched for development, and provide their own atmosphere . . .
>
> AN 95

Here we have Harriet both developing and providing a very different atmosphere. Flat characters are most effective when they are comic; when they are tragic they are a bore. In this case Harriet in the kidnapping incident is certainly not a bore. Her character has shifted, it has become round—with a jolt:

> The test of a round character is whether it is capable of surprising in a convincing way. If it never surprises it is flat. If it does not convince, it is a flat pretending to be round.   AN 106

Harriet's change is surprising, but, I think, convincing. But it is clearly the author's intention not to leave her as a round character. Following the scene in which the carriage is overturned, the baby killed, and Harriet turns from a screaming maniac into a chuckling idiot, she collapses, but 'after a short paroxysm of illness and remorse' quickly returns to her normal state. She will return to Sawston as 'flat' as ever because it is not the author's intention to detract in any way from the real development which has taken place in his more central characters Philip Herriton and Caroline Abbott.

Forster's description of Philip is partly autobiographical:

> His face was plain rather than not, and there was a curious mixture in it of good and bad. He had a fine forehead and a good large nose, and both observation and sympathy were in his eyes. But below the nose and eyes all was confusion, and those people who believe that destiny resides in the mouth and chin shook their heads when they looked at him.   WA 78

Philip too had been bullied and hustled at school and was given to retiring to his cubicle, examining his features in a looking-glass, and sighing. He is of course bullied by his mother and his sister when he is not being bullied by his school-mates. At twenty-two he visited Italy, returning to Sawston a champion of beauty. His impact on that community is negligible.

> He concluded that nothing could happen, not knowing that human love and love of truth sometimes conquer where love of beauty fails.   WA 79

Philip consequently adopts the pose of the disengaged aesthete, to whom life is a spectacle, most often, to laugh at. Events pass him by and he believes he is not one to be changed by circumstances. In both his visits to Italy he is obedient to his mother's wishes but indifferent to the outcome of his missions. Until the death of the child neither human love nor love of truth are within his experience. He is both trivial in his personal relationships and ignorant, through vanity and preoccupation with the figure he himself is cutting, of other people's feelings. The child's death and subsequent happenings prove him to be a man changed by circumstances. He stops posturing, he loses his condescension to Caroline Abbott, and when he thinks she is on the point of declaring her love for him, he discovers that it is Gino she loves. Her reasons for revealing her love to Philip are to him bitterly ironic:

'I dare tell you this because I like you—and because you're without passion; you look on life as a spectacle; you don't enter it; you only find it funny or beautiful. So I can trust you to cure me.' WA 201

In that terrible discovery, Philip managed to think not of himself but of her.

The events at Monteriano have deeply affected both Miss Abbott's and Philip's life, yet neither has been aware of the change in the other, and at a time when Philip is turning from his triviality to the 'love of truth' he is asked to be flippant to allay her anguish.

Miss Abbott and Philip are rounded characters. There are times when they both act surprisingly; they are both certainly changed by circumstances. Philip is transformed from a spectator to a participant by the kidnapping and its consequences; Miss Abbott casts aside her Sawston moral rectitude when for the first time she sees the baby:

The real thing, lying asleep on a dirty rug, disconcerted her. It did not stand for a principle any longer. It was so much flesh and blood, so many inches and ounces of life—a glorious, unquestionable fact, which a man and another woman had given to the world. You could talk to it; in time it would answer you; in time it would not answer you unless it chose, but would secrete, within the compass of its body, thoughts and wonderful passions of its own. And this was the machine on which she and Mrs. Herriton and Philip and Harriet had for the last month been exercising their various ideals—

had determined that in time it should move this way or that way, should accomplish this and not that. It was to be Low Church, it was to be high-principled, it was to be tactful, gentlemanly, artistic—excellent things all. Yet now that she saw this baby, lying asleep on a dirty rug, she had a great disposition not to dictate one of them, and to exert no more influence than there may be in a kiss or in the vaguest of the heartfelt prayers.   WA 145

It is wholly in keeping with Forster's craft that the radical changes effected in his two principal characters should be marked by the two most graphic parts of his story. The first is the way in which Miss Abbott accepts the child as flesh and blood rather than as a principle to be fought for. She accepts at the same time Gino's absolute rights to keep and care for his son. He is about to bath the baby, she asks if she may help him, and together they kneel by the tub, roll up their sleeves, and get on with the job. Miss Abbott soon shows her prowess at bathing babies and Gino takes on the role of attendant.

'I am ready for the soft towel now,' said Miss Abbott, who was strangely exalted by the service.
'Certainly. Certainly.' He strode in a knowing way to a cupboard. But he had no idea where the soft towel was. Generally he dabbed the baby on the first dry thing he found.
'And if you have any powder.'
He struck his forehead despairingly. Apparently the stock of powder was just exhausted.   WA 156

When Philip arrives he sees Miss Abbott sitting on the loggia with a twenty-mile view of the countryside behind her, the naked baby on her knee and Gino standing by in admiration: the Virgin and Child with Donor. It is in that moment of rare harmony that Miss Abbott realises she loves Gino. She runs from the two men weeping bitterly, confused by her own powerful feelings. The bathing of the baby contains the elements of a ritual, but the cleansing rite is not directed solely at the baby. It is Miss Abbott's moment of truth. She has abandoned her Sawston principles; her moral attitudinising has crumpled before the naked baby. Her mind, too, stripped of its protective layers—the insulation of convention—forces on her some stark conclusions. Gino loves his son. Paternity moves strongly in him. That Gino should love his son and, for that reason alone, not wish to part with him, had not for one moment entered the mind of the Herritons, who had anticipated a rapid exchange of the child for not too high a price. Gino's adoration of his son and his elation at the discovery that fatherhood has bestowed on him a measure of immortality, transform him in Miss Abbott's eyes. Her feeling for him is not mistily idealised. She loves him passionately, sensually, and desires him through her to satisfy that deeply felt need for personal continuance.

Philip, however, scorning the Sawston conventions, is protected from life by the insulation of art. On entering the villa, after the bathing episode, he sees not Miss Abbott, the baby, and Gino, but the painting of an Italian Madonna, with her child on her knee, and the rich patron who has commissioned the work of art, kneeling close by. He is looking at a picture not life. Philip Herriton is unable to connect the outer with the inner life, the prose with the passion. Indeed, his mother's persistent 'repression of vigour' has successfully expunged his passion. In him, as in Miss Abbott, the first stirring of true feeling comes when he picks the baby up in his arms. In her, love is unleashed; in him, horror, for when he takes up the child, picking it out of the rut made by the coach wheels, it is dead.

These events which affect Philip deeply occur at the end of the novel. Harriet kidnaps the baby but conceals this fact from Philip until the carriage has crashed and the baby in the darkness and muddle has slipped from her arms. Philip whose elbow is broken gropes through the mud for the child, tries to clean its face from the mud and the rain and the tears.

> He shook the bundle; he breathed into it; he opened his coat and pressed it against him. Then he listened, and heard nothing but the rain and the panting horses, and Harriet who was somewhere chuckling to herself in the dark.   WA 183

Compassion and contrition are new experiences for Philip. He has been unable to save the child and blames himself for his triviality, for the weakness in his own character and he feels it is his duty alone to take the news of the accident to Gino. Gino makes him suffer horribly. He traps him in a dark room and alternatively grates his broken bone in the joint and closes his hand on his windpipe. Miss Abbott intervenes in time to save his life. She separates the two men, brings Gino to his senses, and eases Philip's pain. At this moment Perfetta brings in the milk intended for the baby. Gino collapses sobbing like a child into Miss Abbott's arms.

> Philip looked away, as he sometimes looked away from the great pictures where visible forms suddenly became inadequate for the things they have shown us. He was happy; he was assured there was greatness in the world. There came to him an earnest desire to be good through the example of this good woman. He would try henceforward to be worthy of the things she had revealed. Quietly, without hysterical prayers or banging of drums, he underwent conversion. He was saved.   WA 192

Philip has undergone, in James Joyce's phrase, an epiphany, a sudden spiritual manifestation at this 'delicate and evanescent' moment. This being so, another ritual has to be performed. Miss Abbott asks Gino to give Philip the milk to drink and to finish the rest himself.

> She was determined to use such remnants as lie about the world.
>   WA 193

The libation taken, the jug is smashed, and Gino and Philip have made a communion stronger than death.

Summary
There is in this novel the most delicate artistry. At times it is expressed through a visual image which may convey to the reader the deeper significance of the story. One such example is the bathing of the baby, another is Philip's groping for the baby in the dark and finding it lying across a rut in the road: if the child had fallen into the rut he would not have been found. Sunnier moments are Lilia's first glimpse of Gino sitting on the mud wall opposite the Volterra gate, and Philip and Miss Abbott sharing

the view of Monteriano from the Gothic window of the Stella d'Italia. Views are important to the author, and there is a special significance attached to the blocking of views. The tower from which Philip and Miss Abbott view Monteriano, uninterruptedly, in Philip's words, 'reaches up to heaven and down to the other place. . . . Is it to be a symbol of the town?' In 'Other Kingdom' Miss Beaumont enjoying a picnic in her copse asks Ford to stand so that he blocks the view of the house. Monteriano is full of splendid views whether it is outward to Siena or Poggibonsi or the traces of Giotto within Santa Deodata. When the characters share such splendour there is harmony and deeper understanding.

The first chapter of the novel immediately introduces, with the exception of Gino, the central characters. A send-off from Charing Cross railway station is the occasion of bringing Mrs. Theobald and Mrs. Herriton together, of showing us Mr. Kingcroft's dog-like but ineffectual devotion to Lilia—he arrives with her footwarmer too late—and of Philip in an exuberant mood, exhorting his sister-in-law to love the Italians and to visit the 'little towns—Gubbio, Pienza, Cortona, San Gimignano, Monteriano'. Miss Abbott and Lilia settle down for their journey to Italy, Mrs. Theobald and Mr. Kingcroft return to Yorkshire, and the rest of the chapter is focused on Sawston.

Mrs. Herriton's 'repression of vigour' is felt by all at Sawston, and, on hearing of Lilia's engagement, she intends to make it felt in Italy. The conclusion of the chapter epitomises the defeat of such repression and so introduces in terms of peas and sparrows the novel's central theme. Mrs. Herriton and Harriet have been sowing peas; news comes by letter, which Mrs. Herriton tears up in her anger, of Lilia's engagement; in the subsequent bustle to prevent the marriage the peas are left uncovered. At the end of the day Mrs. Herriton remembers:

> It upset her more than anything, and again and again she struck the
> banisters with vexation. Late as it was, she got a lantern from the
> tool-shed and went down the garden to rake the earth over them.
> The sparrows had taken every one. But countless fragments of the
> letter remained, disfiguring the tidy ground.   25

Lilia, who has escaped Mrs. Herriton's tyranny, lucklessly exchanges one cage for another. Sawston and Monteriano, for so different reasons, can be equally restricting. But, in her blowzy way, she looked to Gino to give her the love and warmth, of which she felt so deprived in Sawston, where all was so tidy, decorous and chilly-hearted. Mrs. Herriton's dominance in her world of 'anger and telegrams' is threatened by Lilia's engagement to an Italian. Philip is therefore summarily dispatched to Monteriano to retrieve the situation, but in vain. Mrs. Herriton's lack of imagination, her will to dominate and to control or crush the personalities of those near to her, in a heartless systematic manner, is epitomised in the sowing of the peas, with such infertile results.

Where Angels Fear to Tread is not a great novel, but it is the work of a fine craftsman who can tell his story with economy of style and gaiety of manner. His ironic temper lightly veils his concern for the human predicament and his belief that writing 'not winged with passion' is worthless. In his first novel, although his canvas is small, Forster has set himself the highest standards; in his later novels he never falls below them.

'THE LONGEST JOURNEY'

Richard Elliot, an hereditary cripple, is known by his friends as Rickie, by his detractors as Rickety. At the outset of the novel he is in his first year at Cambridge mistily following an argument on the existence of objects. Does the cow exist only when there is some one to look at it? The discussion is interrupted by a tall young woman, Agnes Pembroke, entering Rickie's room, scolding him for inviting her brother and herself to Cambridge but forgetting to meet them. Stewart Ansell, the most percipient of the debaters, as he leaves the room ignores Agnes's outstretched hand, explaining later to Rickie that for him she was not there.

For Rickie she is there, and that is his tragedy. Agnes who has known Rickie for many years tells him triumphantly of her engagement to Gerald Dawes. She and her brother Herbert invite Rickie to spend part of his vacation with them, and there for the second time in his life he meets Gerald. The first encounter had taken place when they were boys together at school: Gerald the bully, Rickie the victim:

> ... he and Gerald had met, as it were, behind the scenes, before our decorous drama opens, and there the elder boy had done things to him—absurd things, not worth chronicling separately. An apple-pie bed is nothing; pinches, kicks, boxed ears, twisted arms, pulled hair, ghosts at night, inky books, befouled photographs, amount to very little by themselves. But let them be united and continuous, and you have a hell that no grown-up devil can devise. Between Rickie and Gerald there lay a shadow that darkens life more often than we suppose. The bully and his victim never quite forget their first relations. They meet in clubs and country houses, clap one another on the back; but in both the memory is green of a more strenuous day when they were boys together. LJ 47

Gerald is in the Army and Herbert urges him to make his way in the world before thinking of marrying Agnes. This Gerald accepts although passionate and impatient. Rickie clumsily offers him money so that he could marry. Gerald is outraged at the offer and in his contempt of Rickie reveals to Agnes the tortures he inflicted on him at school.

> For this she scolded him well. But she had a thrill of joy when she thought of the weak boy in the clutches of the strong one. LJ 61

That afternoon Gerald dies 'broken up in the football match'. Rickie shakes Agnes out of her apathy.

> 'It's the worst thing that can ever happen to you in all your life, and you've got to mind it. They'll come saying, "Bear up—trust to time". No, no; they're wrong. Mind it.' LJ 63

At this moment Agnes and Rickie enter a new relationship. Gerald's death has made them interdependent.

Rickie leaves Cambridge with a second class Classics degree. He marries Agnes and together they help Herbert to run his boarding house at Sawston public school. Rickie as a teacher rapidly develops into a martinet, and as a junior housemaster into a cat's-paw for his brother-in-law's petty machinations. At Cambridge Rickie had been prepared to lead a crusade against indifference, the blunting of feeling, the couldn't-care-less attitude. He had insisted passionately that Agnes should let herself feel keenly the loss of Gerald. Now he himself begins to lose the battle against apathy, but he is stung into feeling by the discovery that Stephen Wonham, a dependant of his aunt, Mrs. Failing, is his half-brother. Rickie unquestioningly believes that it is a father they have in common. He is persuaded by Agnes to keep this relationship secret from Stephen. However, Stewart Ansell, his Cambridge friend, on a visit to Sawston meets Stephen, discovers the truth of the relationship, enters the school-house when the boys and the masters are at their Sunday dinner, and in the presence of all accuses Rickie of being ashamed of owning a blood-tie with Stephen, and corrects Rickie's mis-apprehension concerning such a tie. The mother not the father was the common parent.

Stephen returns to Sawston within ten days, drunk and violent. He hurls a brick through the study window.

> Herbert peered into the garden, and a hooligan slipped by him into the house, wrecked the hall, lurched up the stairs, fell against the banisters, balanced for a moment on his spine, and slid over. Herbert called for the police. Rickie who was upon the landing, caught the man by the knees and saved his life. LJ 275

Rickie leaves Agnes and Sawston. He tries to build up a real relationship with Stephen, but with little success:

> He did not love him, even as he had never hated him. In either passion he had degraded him to be a symbol for the vanished past.
> LJ 284

His last act is to push his drunken brother to safety off the rails from the path of a goods train, but to lose his own life in doing so.

The Longest Journey is clearly the most autobiographical of Forster's novels. Cambridge and Sawston are set sharply against each other. The Cambridge cocoon of friendliness, sensitivity and mutual consideration is shed for the self-seeking dominance of Sawston. Cherished hopes and ideals are shattered; the holiness of the heart's affections is desecrated; 'poetry not prose, lies at the core', pleads Rickie. 'Balderdash!' answers his wife.

Some of the author's most painful experiences as a day-boy at Tonbridge gape rawly through the pages of this novel. Herbert Pembroke is almost fanatical in his hatred of day-boys:

> They infect the boarders. Their pestilential, critical, discontented attitude is spreading over the school. LJ 180

His vindictiveness nearly brings about the loss of Varden's life. The boy is mercilessly bullied, morally corrupted by the indoctrination of *esprit de corps*, and physically broken.

Rickie when invited to stay with the Pembrokes is apprehensive of meeting Gerald whom from his school experience he remembers with horror. Yet Gerald derives a sadistic pleasure in recounting to Agnes the details of the tortures enacted on Rickie. Agnes is Gerald's soul-mate and glows at the telling.

Intention to hurt abounds in the novel. Not only in Gerald and Agnes, but in Mrs. Failing who reveals to Rickie Stephen's relationship to him as a savage reprisal. At Rickie's birth his father was sorry that his son's deformity was not greater than his own, and, although more the victim of weak will and misplaced idealism, Rickie is not exempt from this intentional hurting:

> Weakly people, if they are not careful, hate one another, and when the weakness is hereditary the temptation increases. LJ 140

In recent days the Civil Rights marchers in Chicago and San Francisco have remarked on the physical harm they have encountered as insignificant when compared with the overwhelming feeling of hate that has been engendered. Forster understands this distinction:

> There was very little bullying at my school. There was simply the atmosphere of unkindness, which no discipline can dispel. It is not what people do to you, but what they mean that hurts. . . . Physical pain doesn't hurt—at least not what I call hurt—if a man hits you by accident or in play. But just a little tap, when you know it comes from hatred, is too terrible. LJ 192

Stephen, the most violent of the characters in the novel, unseats the soldier from his horse on Salisbury Plain, wrestles with and vanquishes Ansell, throws a brick through Herbert's study window, and crashes through the banisters to what, but for Rickie's catching him, would have been certain death. But it is not in his nature to harm others deliberately nor to harbour a hate which contrives hurting. When at the end of the book his daughter kicks him in the stomach he speaks to her quietly but from the depth of his being:

> 'You tried to hurt me,' he said. 'Hurting doesn't count. Trying to hurt counts.'   LJ 315

Trying to hurt counts to Rickie. From the wretchedness of his school life, the loneliness of his youth in which he would conduct solitary conversations or play Halma against himself, he had escaped to Cambridge which he found so comforting and congenial, so accommodating to the perky, the limp and the odd, that unconsciously burying his hatred for his father he proclaims his affection for all mankind—a romantic exaggeration he is bound to modify when Ansell reminds him of his father. Ansell knows that Rickie's tenuous grasp of reality will be the occasion for inflicting pain on himself and those he loves:

> 'You want to love everyone equally, and that's worse than impossible—it's wrong.'   LJ 27

Ansell treats Agnes as the 'cow that is not there' and ignores her. Naïvely Rickie interprets his behaviour to Agnes as ill-breeding.

> 'Ansell isn't a gentleman. His father's a draper. His uncles are farmers.'

It is a wiser and a sadder Rickie who soon after his marriage realises that his wife bears little resemblance to the symbol of suffering femininity his imagination had created. Ansell's intention is to help Rickie distinguish between the real and the romantic in his feelings for Agnes, his consideration of his friends and parents, and in his relationship with Stephen. It is not surprising that Ansell's fellowship dissertation is 'about things being real' while Rickie's short stories are pure fantasy. It is ironic that the dissertation is rejected while the stories become a posthumous moneyspinner.

These short stories published under the title of *Pan Pipes* resemble in many ways Forster's own work in this genre. 'Other Kingdom' in which the Dryad, Miss Beaumont, engaged to be married to Harcourt Worters, turns into a tree, is similar to the story Rickie outlines to Agnes. But his heroine is repulsed by 'the snobby wedding-presents—and flies out of the drawing-room window, shouting, "Freedom and truth!" Near the house is a little dell full of fir-trees, and she runs into it. He comes there the next moment. But she's gone' (84). She has turned herself into a tree. Agnes is anything but a Dryad and when she comes to the enchanted dell at Madingley she enters it, calls for Rickie to join her and far from changing into a fir-tree ensures that she does not quit the dell until she is engaged to be married. Rickie when he hears her calling drives his fingers into his ears, recognising the voice of the devil, but he is powerless to resist. In his fantasy the Dryad turned herself into a tree to escape human bondage, in reality Agnes invokes the genius of the place to secure such bondage.

The writing of such stories Agnes had at first encouraged, but from thinking them clever she becomes almost derisive:

> How could Rickie or any one make a living by pretending that Greek gods were alive, or that young ladies could vanish into trees? LJ 172

They strike Stephen as equally strange. He leaves the manuscript, charred and smudged, in the gutter on the roof.

Rickie's search for symbols forms part of his addiction to fantasy. On the one hand he exalts Agnes as a symbol of heroic love and masculine fulfilment and on the other Stephen is regarded as a symbol for the vanished past. As the securities of Cambridge fall away he no longer finds such acute pleasure in people. In his mind they move as darker symbols, in his life he withdraws from them. His idealised love for his mother is shattered by the revelation of Stephen's parentage. His exalted notions of human relationship are sharply modified when, as an assistant housemaster, he subserviently intrigues for Herbert and withholds his friendship from his pupils because

... you cannot be friends either with boy or man unless you give yourself away in the process, and Mr. Pembroke did not commend this.   LJ 186

It is out of the sheer weariness of disillusionment that he drags his drunken brother from the railway track and is indifferent to the train running over his own legs.

Agnes persuading Rickie into a speedy marriage says

'If we did marry, we might get to Italy at Easter and escape this horrible fog.'

They marry; they never get to Italy. The fog engulfs them.

The prospect of visiting Italy in the Easter vacation would seem an insufficient motive for a precipitate marriage; yet to this Agnes persuaded Rickie. His compliance marks the change from the cradling of Cambridge to the hazards of Sawston, and in the thickening fog he can never reach back to that moment of contentment at the twilight hour when in his room the discussion on the cow was at a low ebb, the fire had died down, the air was heavy with good tobacco-smoke and the pleasant warmth of tea.

The other philosophers were crouched in odd shapes on the sofa and table and chairs, and one, who was a little bored, had crawled to the piano and was timidly trying the Prelude to Rheingold with his knee upon the soft pedal.   LJ 9–10

Into this scene comes Agnes.

The door opened. A tall young woman stood framed in the light that fell from the passage.

'Ladies!' whispered everyone in great agitation.

'Yes?' he said nervously, limping towards the door (he was rather lame). 'Yes? Please come in. Can I be any good—?'

This is the first we hear of Rickie's lameness. Agnes sees a row of unmatching shoes, boots and pumps and she feels disgust until she is comforted by the remembrance of the perfect physical form of her betrothed, Gerald. Rickie's deformity shared by his father and aunt is hereditary. The analogy with Oedipus is inescapable, especially when we read that Rickie feels he has offended against an Olympian deity, that there is a curse on the house of Elliot that he should have no children. The parents of Oedipus, warned by an oracle that their son should kill his father, give orders that a spike be driven through the child's feet, and that he be exposed to die on Mount Cithaeron. He is found there by a shepherd and brought up in Corinth. But he has been lamed for life. Rickie, too, is lamed for life, and he believes, too, his line is cursed. Ignoring the curse Rickie begets a daughter too terribly deformed to live. Greek themes are deeply imbedded into the story. Ansell repeatedly likens Agnes to Medusa. She is turning Rickie into stone and his only salvation is to avert his eyes and grasp at the Spirit of Life. Rickie on the other hand casts aside his Shelley ('Epipsychidion') to marry Agnes whom he thinks of as 'a kindly Medusa or a Cleopatra with a sense of duty' —at any rate not Greek born and therefore 'barbarian'.

The ultimate disaster at Roman crossing is carefully anticipated in the earlier stages of the novel. Two children were playing on the crossing. Stephen manages to snatch one of them from the path of the oncoming train; the other is killed. Rickie and Agnes are in the train, embracing passionately as it runs over the child. The dialogue between Mrs. Failing and Stephen at Cadover dealing with this accident is compressed and significant:

> 'That reminds me. Another child run over at the Roman crossing. Whish—bang—dead.'
> 'Oh my foot! Oh my foot, my foot!' said Mrs. Failing, and paused to take breath.
> 'Bad?' he asked callously.
> Leighton, with bowed head, passed them with the manuscript and disappeared among the laurels. The twinge of pain, which had been slight, passed away, and they proceeded, descending a green airless corridor which opened into the gravel drive.
> 'Isn't it odd,' said Mrs. Failing, 'that the Greeks should be enthusiastic about laurels—that Apollo should pursue any one who could possibly turn into such a frightful plant? What do you make of Rickie?'   LJ 105–6

The death at Roman crossing is associated with the pain in Mrs. Failing's lame foot. The reader's thought is transferred to Rickie through the mention of laurels which he hopes to win as a young author and through the odd notion that Apollo, symbol of physical perfection, should patronise the misshapen. Rickie's legs are the next offering at Roman crossing.

Chastity and carnal love are in Greek mythology represented respectively by the goddesses Artemis and Aphrodite. Rickie is a fitter devotee of Artemis than Aphrodite. He, however, knows himself too slenderly to worship at the right shrine. The slighted goddess has therefore no intention of carrying out her childbirth duties so far as the safe delivery of his daughter is concerned. Stephen whose instinct is surer devotes himself to Demeter, not consciously of course, but Forster is persistent in this association. Demeter is the goddess of the cornfield who initiates brides and bridegrooms into the secrets of the couch. Forster finds the modern paraphrase of her power 'the survival of the fittest' inadequate, yet something of this sense is in Ansell's mind when he ponders on the opposition of chastity and propagation in the British Museum after hearing that a child is to be born to Rickie and Agnes.

> He left the Parthenon to pass by the monuments of our more reticent beliefs—the temple of Ephesian Artemis, the statue of Cnidian Demeter. Honest, he knew that here were powers he could not cope with, nor, as yet, understand. LJ 206

A picture of the Cnidian Demeter hangs facing the sun-rise, swaying, shimmering and grey, in Stephen's attic at Cadover, a picture that he is careful to take with him when he leaves. As important to him is the faded photograph of Stockholm which had hung in Rickie's rooms at Cambridge and Sawston. The power of Demeter stirs in Stephen as it had once in his parents—in Stockholm.

After Rickie's death Herbert Pembroke leaves Sawston and takes holy orders. Stephen by contrast continues to be responsive to more primitive powers. He has married, he has a daughter, he drinks deep but with candour and without a sense of sin when he hears the call from Dionysus on Mount Cithaeron. For the most part he is earth-bound and earth-sure. His daughter, whom wrapped in a blanket he takes in his arms to spend the night with him on the hill-side, will not come to harm.

Structure

The three parts of the novel, Cambridge, Sawston, Wiltshire, chart Rickie's degeneration. At Cambridge he found sanctuary, friendship, and a will and an ability to write. Sawston shatters his ideals of love, of learning and teaching, above all of personal integrity. He knows that his relationship with both Stewart Ansell and Stephen Wonham has sunk to a shameful compromise. The third part, Wiltshire, contains Rickie's vain attempts to rehabilitate himself. He cuts away from Sawston, from the choking influence of Agnes and Herbert Pembroke. It is ironic that at this stage it is too late for him to be able to form a creative relationship with his half-brother, Stephen. He can only die for him. Thus Wiltshire becomes Rickie's grave, but for Stephen and his family, who have come to terms with themselves and their environment, it promises life and harmony.

Robert, Stephen's father, had been a Wiltshire farmer, and the last section of the novel opens with the account of his elopement to Sweden with Rickie's mother. In the cultivated atmosphere of the Failings' drawing-room he would speak of crops and manure. Rickie's mother sees in him the vitality lacking in the Failings and the Elliots. Her own marriage had been a failure:

> She had asked for facts and had been given 'views', 'emotional standpoints', 'attitudes towards life'. To a woman who believed that facts are beautiful, that the living world is beautiful beyond the laws of beauty, that manure is neither gross nor ridiculous, that a fire, not eternal, glows at the heart of the earth, it was intolerable to be put off with what the Elliots called 'philosophy', and, if she refused, to be told that she had no sense of humour. 'Marrying into the Elliot family.' ... What had they ever done, except say sarcastic things, and limp, and be refined? LJ 261

It is clear from this that Stephen not Rickie would be the son nearest her heart. He lives close to the land: he knows himself, and can dispense, as his mother did, with the Elliot 'philosophy'.

In this context it is interesting to recall Rickie's apology for Ansell's rudeness to Agnes: '. . . his uncles were farmers'.

The Elliots' philosophy gives rise to works of fantasy. The real world is lost or ignored. A significant autobiographical analogy is Forster's account of his childhood friendship for a Hertfordshire farm-lad called Ansell. To this lad Morgan Forster, aged seven, used to retell the adventures of 'The Swiss Family Robinson', and expect Ansell to repeat what he had heard. Of this task the farm-hand made heavy weather, but through their companionship and their games Forster admits that 'he did more than anyone towards armouring me against life' (MT 275).

The novel, in its three parts, moves from the philosophy of the existence of objects, discussed in Rickie's Cambridge rooms in the opening chapter, through the central section of compromise, in which the Elliot philosophy is exposed in all its inadequacies, to the third section which ends with Stephen, a farmer's natural son, sleeping under the stars with his daughter, confident 'that he guided the future of our race, and that century after century, his thoughts and his passions would triumph in England'.

SUMMARY

The novel abounds with autobiographical material which at times obtrudes to the detriment of the aesthetic effect. The dominance of the Greek themes is contrived rather than organic. The appearance of Pan and the tales of fantasy are a throw-back to the author's less mature achievement. The dell at Madingley, Rickie's sanctuary and the scene of his seduction, looms as a symbol of Freudian significance, as does the Roman crossing, where on one occasion he passionately embraces Agnes, and on another the train cuts off his legs and he dies. Stewart Ansell's harangue to the Sawston boys at their Sunday dinner strains credibility. This public exposure of Rickie, bringing with it the revelation of Rickie's true relationship to Stephen Wonham, has more than a tc ..ch of Greek tragedy about it. The shock of Gerald's death and the convenience of Robert's, make the reader uneasy about the author's intentions. Is this melodrama, tragedy or comedy, or is it all, muddled together? It certainly contains elements of all, but it is not muddled. It has a design, worked out for the most part with subtlety and imagination. This novel will retain its power because it is written from a poetic impulse to catch the frustration and muddle that beset an artist, who, in his youth, has to make his way unaided, from fantasy to reality, from ignorance to self-knowledge.

4

Fiction II

Structure

A Room with a View published in 1908 is a novel in two parts. Part I takes place in Italy and Part II in England. The first part might be described as the impact of the English on the English in Italy; the second as the impact of Italy on the English in England. The first part though set in Italy contains no Italian characters of more than incidental significance. The Italy we encounter is drastically anglicised. The Pension Bertolini is run by a Cockney Signora who hangs portraits of Queen Victoria and the Poet Laureate in the dining-room and contrives to impart to the drawing-room 'the solid comfort of a Bloomsbury boarding-house'. Among its clientèle the class issues are as keenly felt as in an English hotel. The manner in which the Emersons offer their rooms to Miss Bartlett and Lucy betrays them as ill-bred. Miss Bartlett

> looked around as much as to say, 'Are you all like this?' And two little old ladies, who were sitting farther up the table, with shawls hanging over the backs of the chairs, looked back, clearly indicating 'We are not; we are genteel'. RV 11

The visit to Santa Croce opposes two English views of its art treasures. The Reverend Cuthbert Eager extols its medievalism, while Mr. Emerson scoffs at the fresco depicting a fat man in blue, shooting 'into the sky like an air-balloon'. Eager is the resident chaplain for the English community. It is a point of pride for him that he should distinguish for the tourists the superiority of the residents:

He knew the people who never walked about with Baedekers, who had learnt to take a siesta after lunch, who took drives the pension tourists had never heard of, and saw by private influence galleries which were closed to them. Living in delicate seclusion, some in furnished flats, others in Renaissance villas on Fiesole's slope, they read, wrote, studied, and exchanged ideas, thus attaining to that intimate knowledge, or rather perception, of Florence which is denied to all who carry in the pockets the coupons of Cook.   RV 64

It is apparent that Mr. Eager, conscious of the advantages he enjoys, seeks to impress the less fortunate tourists with his knowledge and artistic perception. He is certainly more successful in impressing the English than the Italians. However, he no more impresses the Emersons, who knew him when he was a curate in Brixton, than the Italian photograph vendor and carriage driver. They are emancipated from his cultural and class snobbishness because their thought and action are not encumbered by English middle-class conventions. The Emersons resemble the Italians in their forthrightness and honesty in emotional response. The love-making of the driver and his inamorata shocks the English, who are nevertheless prepared to tolerate such free and open embraces because the lovers are Italian; but Miss Bartlett believes she snatches Lucy from the bottomless abyss when she interrupts George kissing her among the violets.

It would seem that nothing short of a traumatic experience can move Lucy to begin to think or feel honestly. An Italian is stabbed to death a few feet away from her in the Piazza Signoria. His blood stains her packet of photographs. She faints, falls, and is rescued by George Emerson. The Italian's death brings them close together.

It was not exactly that a man had died; something had happened to the living.   RV 59

The next Italian to bring them together is the driver of the carriage taking the English party into the hills overlooking Florence. She asks him to take her to the *buoni homini* (the good men). The driver, giving a personal interpretation, leads her to George. It is from the ensuing embrace that she is snatched by the vigilant Miss Bartlett, and subsequently persuaded to leave the renaissance snares of Florence for the classical calm of Rome.

The second part of the novel, set in England, begins with a chapter entitled 'Medieval'. It introduces Cecil whom Lucy has promised to marry.

> He was medieval. Like a Gothic statue. Tall and refined, with shoulders that seemed braced square by an effort of will, and a head that was tilted a little higher than the usual level of vision, he resembled those fastidious saints who guard the portals of a French cathedral. Well educated, well endowed, and not deficient physically, he remained in the grip of a certain devil whom the modern world knows as self-consciousness, and whom the medieval, with dimmer vision, worshipped as asceticism. A Gothic statue implies celibacy, just as a Greek statue implies fruition.   RV 106

It was the medieval, in this sense, in Lucy that encouraged her to escape from George Emerson. The structure of the novel, in its two parts, reflects the dominance of a medieval asceticism in the first part overcome by a joyous renaissance in the second. The last chapter is entitled 'The End of the Middle Ages', but to achieve this 'End' Lucy hazards her happiness in self-deception. The chapters leading up to the last are entitled 'Lying to George', 'Lying to Cecil', 'Lying to Mr. Beebe ...', 'Lying to Mr. Emerson'. She discovers in Mr. Emerson not a medieval but a modern saint and she responds to his call:

> 'we fight for more than Love or Pleasure: there is Truth'.

She gives up her plan to go to Greece, another classical escape route, marries George against the wishes of her mother, and returns with him to their room with a view in Florence. As they look out of the window a cabman offers them repeatedly his services. The street vendor troubling Mr. Eager is recalled by the reader. Lucy in love is a match for the cabman. She appeals to his Italian heart

> 'Signorina, domani faremo uno giro—'
> Lucy bent forward and said with gentleness:
> 'Lascia, prego, lascia. Siamo sposati.'

'Scusi tanto, signora,' he replied, in tones as gentle, and whipped up his horse.   RV 255

Lucy's warmth and directness find the like response from the cabman. She has achieved a dialogue which will always evade the Reverend Cuthbert Eager in his encounters with the Italian peasantry. Old Mr. Emerson had shown Lucy 'the holiness of direct desire' and she had found strength and courage enough to cast aside the Middle Ages, the close tutelage of parent, priest and chaperon, and move into her renaissance.

Class

Places are contrasted less in this novel than people. In *The Longest Journey* and *Where Angels Fear to Tread* Sawston, Cambridge and Italy have power to sway personal judgment and action. Such places assume in the novels symbolic significance. At the outset of *A Room with a View* it is clear that the novelist is concerned less with the impact of place on people—the *pension* in Florence might be mistaken for a Bloomsbury guest-house—and more with the contrasting of class and ideological differences.

The manners of the Emersons shock the English residents of the Pension Bertolini. Their forthrightness, honesty and unselfishness is a further cause for embarrassment. The most tolerant of the Emersons is Mr. Beebe, but even he is disconcerted:

'It is so difficult—at least, I find it difficult—to understand people who speak the truth.'   RV 16

The Emersons approach life and art through the senses. Mr. Eager's approach is through the spirit. When they confront Giotto's work they are understandably at odds. Mr. Eager directs his fellow countrymen

'To worship Giotto, not by tactile valuations, but by the standards of the spirit.'   RV 23

Old Mr. Emerson quotes Housman, and among his books are found the works of Gibbon, Samuel Butler, Schopenhauer and Nietzsche. There is a delicate irony in so scholarly a clergyman as Mr. Beebe not having heard of Butler's anti-clerical *The Way of*

64

All Flesh. The Emersons' radical beliefs on religion, ethics and art are as unacceptable as their crude manners, humble origin, and association with the railway.

> Miss Bartlett had asked Mr. George Emerson what his profession was, and he had answered 'the railway'. She was very sorry she had asked him. She had no idea it would be such a dreadful answer, or she would not have asked him.   RV 82

To Miss Lavish they are a source of mirth and derision. George she imagines she has seen as a porter on the South-Eastern. Cecil also finds them quaint and amusing. He comes across them in the Umbrian Room of the National Gallery

> admiring Luca Signorelli—of course, quite stupidly.   RV 142

With crushing condescension he uses them to gain a casual personal advantage:

> 'What a chance of scoring off Sir Harry! and I took their address and a London reference, found they weren't actual blackguards— it was great sport—'   RV 143

The sport is short-lived for Cecil and is, in part, the reason for Lucy breaking off her engagement with him. She realises that between Cecil and George there is not just a difference in class but a difference in vigour, mental and physical. Cecil looks back, George looks forward. The former is encrusted with medievalism, the latter—railwayman that he is—works for the future. Cecil is effete: too weary to make up a four at tennis. His first attempt to embrace Lucy is disastrous.

> As he approached her he found time to wish that he could recoil. As he touched her, his gold pince-nez became dislodged and was flattened between them.   RV 132

George not only plays tennis well; he plays to win. No pince-nez hinders his passionate and unpremeditated kissing of Lucy. His marriage with Lucy offends her family and her class but it gives the world more honesty, passion and vigour.

Cecil is medieval in his self-consciousness, his asceticism, and his inclination towards celibacy. Mr. Beebe had discerned Cecil's inclinations and knew, far from being happily married to Lucy, Cecil would be better detached. Mr. Beebe himself would never marry.

> His belief in celibacy, so reticent, so carefully concealed beneath his tolerance and culture, now came to the surface and expanded like a flower. 'They that do marry do well, but they that refrain do better.' So ran his belief, and he never heard that an engagement was broken off but with a slight feeling of pleasure. RV 229

In the Pension Bertolini there are many single ladies, most of them too old to hope to marry. For Lucy who is young enough to hope for both love and marriage there is the vigilant protection offered by her cousin, Miss Bartlett, who, in repeatedly frustrating any development in the relationship between George and Lucy, would seem to be, like Mr. Beebe, a champion of celibacy. Her situation and beliefs are, however, radically different. Her duty as a chaperon is to return Lucy to her mother as chaste as when she set out, and to ensure in the process that Lucy is not exposed to the attentions of any undesirable young men. Her assiduity is such that in her protectiveness she increases Lucy's interest in George. When in the second part of the book she asks for houseroom at Lucy's home, because her boiler has broken down, she is indirectly responsible for Lucy breaking off her engagement with Cecil. It would appear furthermore, from the dialogue in the last chapter, that she contrived the meeting between Lucy and Mr. Emerson at Mr. Beebe's—the crucial meeting at which Lucy swept aside her self-deception and from the old man took courage to be herself.

> He had robbed the body of its taint, the world's taunts of their sting; he had shown her the holiness of direct desire. She 'never exactly understood', she would say in after years, 'how he managed to strengthen her. It was as if he had made her see the whole of everything at once.' RV 250

Mr. Beebe is a celibate by nature and principle. Miss Bartlett is not. Indeed her nature and principles bring about Lucy's marriage. She is present when George with passion tells Lucy of his love. Lucy is not the only one moved. She is not alone in sensing the imminence of a seasonal change in her life. George had pleaded for the recognition of youth and love:

'It is being young. . . . It is being certain that Lucy cares for me really. It is that love and youth matter intellectually.'　　RV 205

When he has gone Lucy moves out of the house.

But, once in the open air, she paused. Some emotion—pity, terror, love, but the emotion was strong—seized her, and she was aware of autumn. Summer was ending, and the evening brought her odours of decay, the more pathetic because they were reminiscent of spring. That something or other mattered intellectually? A leaf, violently agitated, danced past her, while other leaves lay motionless. That the earth was hastening to re-enter darkness, and the shadows of those trees to creep over Windy Corner?　　RV 206

The following spring Lucy returns to her room with a view in Florence with George as her husband. She has acknowledged her youth and her love and in so doing achieved an intellectual honesty. George had unwittingly prepared himself for this spring-rite by rescuing Lucy when she had fainted on seeing the murdered Italian, by his embracing her at that enchanted meeting among the violets, and by his baptism in the pond from which he emerged to confront Mrs. Honeychurch, Lucy and Cecil, naked apart from his wearing Mr. Beebe's hat, a widewake. This hilarious yet deeply moving chapter (XII) ends with a hint at its ritualistic significance.

It had been a call to the blood and to the relaxed will, a passing benediction whose influence did not pass, a holiness, a spell, a momentary chalice for youth.　　RV 163

The novel ends with the completion of the rite: love, marriage and a return to Florence. This time, however, the lovers share the view: it is fresh to them both, reassuring them of their love and their youth as they look out on to the Arno on that evening in spring.

Pattern

The novel begins with Helen Schlegel's letter to her sister. She writes from Howards End, a Hertfordshire country house, where she is staying as the guest of the Wilcox family. She falls in love with the house and, for a spell, the family. The house continues to hold a strong attraction for her and later for her sister, Margaret, who by marrying Henry Wilcox becomes its mistress. The novel ends with the Schlegel sisters firmly ensconced at Howards End. On Margaret's death the property will pass to her nephew, Helen's son.

Paradoxically, the Wilcoxes, who are property conscious, with sharp and unscrupulous acquisitive characteristics, find themselves dispossessed; whereas the Schlegels, who are dilatory and casual in their business transactions, become the inheritors. The novel, however, is scarcely concerned with business transactions; even less with a struggle for property. Howards End signifies more than a house in the country; it becomes a symbol of personal freedom and hope for the future. It is to belong to those who can cherish it.

Ruth Wilcox had both owned and cherished Howards End. She had intended giving it as a Christmas present to Margaret Schlegel. On her death-bed she bequeathed it to Margaret, who remained for many years ignorant of both the intended Christmas present and the ultimate bequest. Margaret, Mrs. Wilcox knew intuitively, would cherish Howards End. She would love and respect the wych-elm and the silver birches; no more paddocks would be turned into garages; at Howards End the Schlegels would be spiritually at home.

From Helen's first visit to the time of her return, when she has been lured to Howards End and trapped there, her view of the Wilcoxes is that they are the resourceful hunters, the empire-builders, the champions of impersonal forces, fearful of the inner life and suspicious of foreigners. She withdraws dismayed from their familiar 'outer life of telegrams and anger' to her own inner life which rests on the belief in the importance of personal relations.

Her friendship for Leonard Bast, and the child she bears, are testimony of this belief. But her championship of the Basts borders on the fanatical because of her disgust at the Wilcoxes, a disgust that is fiercely intensified when she discovers that at one time Mrs. Bast was Henry Wilcox's kept woman, and that his casual, impersonal advice concerning Leonard's employment prospects results in disastrous poverty for the Basts. Helen thinks more generously of Leonard Bast than she does of the Wilcoxes because both she and her sister detect in him an essential quality lacking in the Wilcoxes.

> 'He's vulgar and hysterical and bookish, but don't think that sums him up. There's manhood in him as well. Yes, that's what I'm trying to say. He's a real man.' (156) HE 156

It is not that the Schlegels are here redefining manhood, but rather that they respect Leonard Bast in his quest for a richer life. His Sunday walk through the night to meet the Surrey dawn touches their imagination. He may one day link his daily life with the husks of his reading.

> 'We wanted to help you; we also supposed you might help us. We did not have you here out of charity—which bores us—but because we hoped there would be a connection between last Sunday and other days. What is the good of your stars and trees, your sunrise and the wind, if they do not enter into our daily lives? They have never entered into mine, but into yours ...' HE 151

For the Wilcoxes Helen, after her first encounter with them, has nothing but scorn. They may succeed as pig-sticking colonialists abroad, as pillars of trade and commerce at home, they may show their zest for games and their skill with motor-cars, but because they shun the inner life, because they pursue the impersonal and avoid the use of 'I', they fail to attest their manhood. Ruth

69

Wilcox's written wish to leave Howards End to Margaret Schlegel is ignored.

> They did neglect a personal appeal. The woman who had died did say to them, 'Do this,' and they answered, 'We will not.' HE 104

Henry Wilcox's affair with Mrs. Bast did not touch his conscience because 'poor old Ruth had never found him out'. He proved unfaithful to her while she was living, and after she died. The eventual reversion of Howards End to Margaret Schlegel occurs only when, crushed by events, Henry Wilcox has some understanding of his own moral failure.

The Wilcoxes and the Schlegels meet for the first time in Germany. Both families are on holiday, they meet on an expedition, and Ruth Wilcox on her return to England invites the sisters to Howards End. Meg stays with their sick brother, Tibby. Helen goes alone to Howards End.

The Schlegels' father was a German who, having fought in the Franco-Prussian war, forsook Germany to become a naturalised Englishman, teaching in one of the provincial universities. The rapid growth of the German empire dismayed him. He expostulated to a haughty nephew against both Pan-Germanism and British imperialism:

> 'It is the vice of a vulgar mind to be thrilled by bigness, to think that a thousand square miles are a thousand times more wonderful than one square mile, and that a million square miles are almost the same as heaven. That is not imagination. No, it kills it. When their poets over here try to celebrate bigness they are dead at once, and naturally. Your poets too are dying, your philosophers, your musicians to whom Europe has listened for two hundred years. Gone. Gone with the little courts that nurtured them—' HE 30–1

Margaret and Helen, his daughters, are true to these sentiments. They exalt literature and the arts above any concern for nationalism or public life. Their interest in politics is considerable but in their idealism 'they desired that public life should mirror whatever is good in the life within'. Music is a key to the enchanted land of the imagination. But here their delight falls short of

'Pomp and Circumstance'. Even the parties they attend are of a philosophic nature at which earnest 'papers' are read.

The Schlegels' house in Wickham Place, a leasehold property, was left them by their father. At the expiration of this lease, they will not only lose their home, but the house in Wickham Place will be demolished to make way for the development of blocks of flats. The family is rootless and homeless. They are all three left comfortable incomes: their English-born mother was wealthy enough. Margaret, however, is indecisive in her search for a new home, and it is at this stage that she approaches Henry Wilcox, rather lightly, to seek his advice. Not given to half measures, Henry Wilcox offers her his home and his hand.

Margaret's marriage, which is met with the joint disapproval of the Schlegels and the Wilcoxes, is an earnest endeavour on Margaret's part to bridge the gap between the outer life of telegrams and anger and the inner life of personal relations. She fails, and in her failure her integrity is compromised. She takes part in the trapping and hunting down of her sister; but the moment she realises that Helen is pregnant she is prepared to defend her against the world. She is too late, however, to prevent the Wilcoxes hunting down Leonard Bast. Charles kills him. The verdict of manslaughter crushes his father, who goes to pieces; and Margaret, in kindness rather than love, looks after him at Howards End, where the ménage is soon to be increased by the birth of Helen's son.

The novel opposes and contrasts two ideologies. The attempt to link them ends in disaster. The birth of the child brings hope; but hope for Helen's world—a world without compromise. Margaret owns Howards End and this becomes her nephew's inheritance. It is all part of the final harvest which Helen and her baby share.

> 'The field's cut!' Helen cried excitedly—'the big meadow! We've seen to the very end, and it'll be such a crop of hay as never!'
>
> HE 362

'Only connect . . .'

Margaret Schlegel had hoped for a different harvest, at which Wilcoxes and Schlegels might have rejoiced together. It was her vision to link the prose and passion of life, and it was in the hope of building such a rainbow bridge that she married Henry Wilcox.

> 'Only connect!' That was the whole of her sermon. Only connect the prose and the passion, and both will be exalted, and human love will be seen at its height.　　　　　　　　　　　　　HE 197

It is given to few to see life steadily and see it whole. Henry Wilcox sees it steadily; Margaret believes she sees it whole. Henry's steady gaze wavers momentarily when confronted by Mrs. Bast, his former mistress, but he is incapable of seeing any connection between his own misconduct and Helen's. Margaret at her most passionate tries to enlighten him:

> 'You shall see the connection if it kills you, Henry! You have had a mistress—I forgave you. My sister has a lover—you drive her from the house. Do you see the connection? Stupid, hypocritical, cruel— oh, contemptible!—a man who insults his wife when she's alive and cants with her memory when she's dead. A man who ruins a woman for his pleasure, and casts her off to ruin other men. And gives bad financial advice, and then says he is not responsible. These men are you. You can't recognise them, because you cannot connect. I've had enough of your unweeded kindness. I've spoilt you long enough. All your life you have been spoiled. Mrs. Wilcox spoiled you. No one has ever told what you are—muddled, criminally muddled. Men like you use repentance as a blind, so don't repent. Only say to yourself, "What Helen has done, I've done".'　　　　　　HE 325

Leonard Bast, with all his shortcomings, is more self-aware, more prepared to scrutinise his own conduct, and to journey to Howards End to say 'Mrs. Wilcox, I have done wrong'. It is for this quality that Margaret regards him as 'a real man'. Henry hides himself behind an incomplete asceticism. His 'sneaking belief that bodily passion is bad' is exemplified by the suddenness with which he snatches his first kiss from his bride-to-be:

72

> ... when it was over he saw her safely to the door and rang the bell
> for her, but disappeared into the night before the maid answered
> it ... he had hurried away as if ashamed, and for an instant she was
> reminded of Helen and Paul.   HE 194

Helen's most awful memory of the Wilcox family was at the
breakfast table, the morning after Paul had proposed to her: the
family placid in their ignorance, Paul terrified at his impulsive
action. Impulse and passion are wretched impediments to the
progress of motor-cars, out-door games and business concerns.

Margaret, however, cannot blind herself to the Wilcox virtues
of

> neatness, decision, and obedience, virtues of the second rank, no
> doubt, but they formed our civilisation.   HE 109

She believes that the Schlegels, who live on their investments,
should value the virtues that establish and keep intact that civilisation. Money she regards as the warp of civilisation:

> independent thoughts are in nine cases out of ten the result of
> independent means.   HE 135

The woof is what one chooses; the satisfaction of one's heart's
desire. For Leonard Bast it might be walking at night; for Tibby,
Oxford; for Mrs. Wilcox, Howards End.

Chapter V, which begins with an account of the Schlegels and
their friends responding in their various ways to a performance
of Beethoven's Fifth Symphony at the Queen's Hall, is strategic-
ally placed. It follows the fiasco of Helen's abortive engagement,
in which the romance and heroism of the evening were replaced
by panic and emptiness in the morning: and it introduces
Leonard Bast, the insurance clerk. After some deliberation he
has paid two shillings for a ticket and he finds himself sitting next
to Margaret Schlegel. He is almost crushed by the consciousness
of his own inadequacies. Can he afford a programme? Dare he
give the Schlegels his address or, having stolen his umbrella, will
they raid his flat and take away his cane as well? Is it 'Tannhouser'
or 'Tannhoyser'? 'Better not risk the word.' He must prepare his

sentences carefully before speaking. He is more concerned to improve his mind than to give himself to a great work of art. Beethoven's music might move him, but his impulse is to look along the row first before committing himself.

Helen's response to the symphony is to translate it into verbal terms. There are heroes and shipwrecks in the first movement, and heroes, elephants dancing and goblins in the third movement. The goblins are ominous: they question whether there is any such thing as splendour or heroism in the world. In the music they are vanquished, but they might return.

Leonard Bast hurries away from Wickham Place, refusing to take tea with the Schlegels, humiliated by Helen's unwitting reference to his umbrella as 'it's gone along the seams. It's an appalling umbrella.' Helen, Margaret and Aunt Juley are strangely impressed by the incident.

> It remained as a goblin footfall, as a hint that all is not for the best in the best of all possible worlds, and that beneath these superstructures of wealth and art there wanders an ill-fed boy, who has recovered his umbrella indeed, but who has left no address behind him, and no name.　　　　　　　　　　　　　　　　　HE 47

This is a masterly introduction of Leonard Bast. He and his wife are caught up with both the Schlegels and the Wilcoxes. The goblin footfall is there, but in Leonard Bast there is a touch of heroism too. The symphony connects with the story. When Helen's child takes 'the great chances of beauty and adventure that the world offers', he will hear with his mother 'the gusts of splendour, the heroism, the youth, the magnificence of life and death' in Beethoven's music. The courage muted in his father may speak through him.

Mythology

> Dickinson loved England, he felt its scenery to be trembling on the verge of an exquisite mythology which only Shakespeare has evoked and he only incidentally. Despite our vile climate and the increasing vileness of our towns he kept a vision of sunlight, water, hedgerows, flowers and the names of flowers. These last—though he frequently forgot them—were an earnest of our native poetry, he

thought; speedwell and traveller's joy represent something which has scarcely found entrance into our literature, and not at all into our lives.   GLD 67

Howards End trembles on the verge of an exquisite mythology. Margaret Schlegel returning to Howards End for the second time is deeply moved by the Hertfordshire scenery. The author asks

> 'Why has not England a great mythology? Our folklore has never advanced beyond daintiness, and the greater melodies about our countryside have all issued through the pipes of Greece. Deep and true as the native imagination can be, it seems to have failed here. It has stopped with the witches and the fairies. It cannot vivify one fraction of a summer field, or give names to half a dozen stars. England still waits for the supreme moment of her literature—for the great poet who shall voice her, or, better still, for the thousand little poets whose voice shall pass into our common talk.'   HE 282

Forster is neither 'the great poet' nor one of 'the thousand little poets', but he has recognised, as Dickinson, the need for a mythology, and within his own experience, he has recreated in this novel a mysticism which can only be successfully communicated through myth. If the indigenous myth is lacking, the communication stumbles. In such a context the pipes of Greece are useless. This novel is about a home in Hertfordshire, and about some of the people who have lived and will live in that home, and will cherish it. Howards End is an essential part of England. Margaret's first visit to her future home alerts her to this relationship.

> She forgot the luggage and the motor-cars, and the hurrying men who know so much and connect so little. She recaptured the sense of space, which is the basis of all earthly beauty, and, starting from Howards End, she attempted to realise England. She failed—visions do not come when we try, though they may come through trying. But an unexpected love of the island awoke in her, connecting on this side with the joys of the flesh, and on that with the inconceivable. Helen and her father had known this love, poor Leonard Bast was groping after it, but it had been hidden from Margaret till this afternoon. It had certainly come through the house and old Miss

Avery. Through them: the notion of 'through' persisted; her mind trembled towards a conclusion which only the unwise have put into words.   HE 216

After Ruth Wilcox's death it is Miss Avery who appears on Margaret's first and second visits to Howards End. Her first appearance is as a ghost out of the past. Margaret momentarily believes she is Mrs. Wilcox, and faints. For Margaret's second visit the Schlegels' furniture and books, contrary to instructions, have been unpacked and have been placed with extraordinary propriety in the nooks and crannies of Howards End. Miss Avery is as a brooding spirit willing the succession of the house from one Mrs. Wilcox to another. The second Mrs. Wilcox, however, is expected to make Howards End the home for her brother and sister also. Their belongings have also been unpacked and carefully placed. Miss Avery herself by marrying Howard Wilcox might have become the owner of the house. Howard was killed, the house passed to Ruth Wilcox, and it was her wish that the house should pass to Margaret Schlegel. Miss Avery becomes an instrument of this wish. Howards End, as England, must pass to those who will cherish it. Their destinies become indistinguishable. Watching the tide turn in Poole Harbour, Margaret Schlegel ponders on England's inheritance.

England was alive, throbbing through all her estuaries, crying for joy through the mouths of all her gulls, and the north wind, with contrary motion, blew stronger against her rising seas. What did it mean? For what end are her fair complexities; her changes of soil, her sinuous coast? Does she belong to those who have moulded her and made her feared by other lands, or to those who have added nothing to her power, but have somehow seen her, seen the whole island at once, lying as a jewel in a silver sea, sailing as a ship of souls, with all the brave world's fleet accompanying her towards eternity.   HE 185

Howards End, as England, will belong to the Schlegels and not the Wilcoxes. If England had its mythology Howards End would be personified as a central character. There is magic and mystery in the house. It opens its door to Margaret Schlegel, but appears locked to Henry Wilcox (212). It accommodates the Schlegels' furniture whereas the Wilcoxes' spills over. The wych-elm shows its pigs' teeth to Margaret but never to Henry Wilcox. The wych-elm whose power is apparently diminishing could not only cure the toothache, if its bark were chewed,

> It could cure anything—once.   HE 75

The wych-elm and the house have an interdependent existence:

> It was a comrade, bending over the house, strength and adventure in its roots, but in its utmost fingers tenderness. . . . Their message was not of eternity, but of hope on this side of the grave.   HE 218

Ruth Wilcox, who tends with loving care the garden at Howards End, watching in the early morning the opening of the large red poppies, has no fear of the grave. Compared with her passion for Howards End death is insignificant, and by her deep intuitive powers she knows that her passion will live on in Margaret and Helen. She comes of Quaker stock and draws spiritual strength from an inward light. Margaret's friends find her dull: she is neither clever nor even alert, yet 'her personality transcended their own and dwarfed their activities'. Ruth Wilcox exists in a different dimension from the other characters.

> She and daily life were out of focus. . . . And at lunch she seemed more out of focus than usual, and nearer the line that divides daily life from a life that may be of greater importance.   HE 80

Like Mrs. Moore, in *A Passage to India*, she possesses a still, hidden power, and like Mrs. Moore she exerts an influence on others wholly incommensurate with her apparent personality. Mrs. Moore takes on after her death a mythical significance; Mrs. Wilcox continues to exert her will through Miss Avery and the Schlegels, through the magical wych-elm and the house itself. The rust of London may be encroaching on the Hertford-shire countryside, the architecture of hurry may be demolishing long-established homes, such as Wickham Place, and replacing them with soaring impersonal flats, but while Mrs. Wilcox's spirit has power, the countryside will not yield to the city; garden, field and meadow will remain precious and pertinent to those men and women who, forsaking the hurry and the zest for mobility, look for their happiness in a home in which they can live and die.

5

Fiction III

A Passage

In the novel a passage to India is a non-event. It does not happen. Mrs. Moore tries to leave India, but dies before the ship has barely left Bombay, and is buried in the Indian Ocean. Fielding, after the fracas of the court case, leaves India for a time. He reappears in the story inspecting the English education offered in the remoter states of Central India. No mention is made of his return passage.

The novel comprises a complex study of relationships, individual and communal, between the English and the Indians. Adela Quested's vain plea to see the *real* India is met by Turton's ineffectual Bridge Party. In the event there is neither bridge nor passage between the English and the Indians. The English institutions preclude any personal approach. When the demands of the institutions are set aside, communion becomes possible. Respect and friendship grow from the meeting of Mrs. Moore and Aziz in the mosque; Aziz allows Fielding to look at the photograph of his dead wife; and Fielding, in flouting the English club conventions by not joining the phalanx of the whites against the 'niggers', establishes the sanctity and sanity of a personal relationship with an Indian in the teeth of the hysteria and viciousness shown collectively by both English and Indians.

The friendship of Aziz and Fielding is deep but not lasting. There are forces that pull them apart: Aziz's suspicions about Fielding's motives for persuading him not to claim damages from Miss Quested; Fielding's marriage to Stella and his subsequent alignment with the Establishment. He can then no longer boast of travelling lightly. They are pulled apart, too, by India itself, with its diversity of races and religions, a country that could only feel united in its hatred of the English. On their last ride together they know that however much *they* wish it their hope of a continuing friendship is frail:

> But the horses didn't want it—they swerved apart; the earth didn't want it, sending up rocks through which riders must pass single file; the temples, the tank, the jail, the palace, the birds, the carrion, the Guest House, that came into view as they issued from the gap and saw Mau beneath: they didn't want it, they said in their hundred voices, 'No, not yet,' and the sky said, 'No, not there'.　　PI 336

The friendships between Aziz and Fielding, and Aziz and Mrs. Moore are in a sense successful 'passages'. There are others, more submerged.

Following their experiences in the Marabar caves Adela Quested and Mrs. Moore find that they can communicate with each other telepathically. Adela knows that Mrs. Moore thinks Aziz innocent before she in fact says so. They share the affliction of the echo, but Mrs. Moore suffers the additional pain of knowing what it means. When Adela thinks lucidly her echo disappears, and it is by thinking of Mrs. Moore that lucidity comes.

Mrs. Moore's telepathic sense is hinted at earlier. When Adela recounts the details of the accident in the Nawab Bahadur's car,

> Mrs. Moore shivered, 'A ghost!' But the idea of a ghost scarcely passed her lips.　　PI 101

Later in the evening Adela questions Mrs. Moore about the anxiety she, Adela, has felt about her engagement to Ronny.

> 'You mean that my bothers are mixed up with India?'
> 'India's—' She stopped.
> 'What made you call it a ghost?'
> 'Call what a ghost?'
> 'The animal thing that hit us. Didn't you say "Oh, a ghost," in passing?'

> 'I couldn't have been thinking of what I was saying.'
> 'It was probably a hyena, as a matter of fact.'
> 'Ah, very likely.'   PI 103

The Nawab Bahadur nine years ago had driven his car over a drunken man and killed him 'and the man had been waiting for him ever since'. 'The animal thing' is the dead man's spirit in 'unspeakable form' haunting the scene of the original accident. The Nawab's second accident brings Adela and Ronny closer together by engendering in them both an animal warmth. Albeit all they do is hold hands in the back of the car, these soft pressures, applied and received, clinch their engagement. Adela inspects the tracks on the road, and she sees similar tracks on the rock footholds before she enters the fateful Marabar caves. On that later occasion as she recognises the similarity of the tracks, she realises that her engagement is based merely on an animal impulse. She questions Aziz about love and marriage with such insensitivity that he escapes from her into the nearest cave, and she, ignorant of his confusion, follows at leisure into what she thinks is the same cave.

The echo in the caves reduces all sound to 'boum'. Mrs. Moore's experience is terrifying and she struggles out of the cave believing at first that she had been physically assaulted. She subsequently lapses into a state 'where the horror of the universe and its smallness are both visible at the same time'. She dully apprehends the insignificance of man.

> What dwelt in the first of the caves? Something very old and very small. Before time, it was before space also.   PI 217

The Marabar hills are older than anything in the world. 'To call them "uncanny" suggests ghosts, and they are older than all spirit.' As such they are beyond the apprehension of even Mrs. Moore.

The caves, in a way, unite Mrs. Moore, Adela Quested and Aziz, but affect them in radically different ways. Mrs. Moore lapses into apathy, Adela's reason is unsettled, Aziz comes to believe that he invited disaster 'because he had challenged the spirit of the Indian earth, which tries to keep men in compartments'.

Their experience in the caves precipitates the breakdown of reasonable communication between the English and the Indians at Chandrapore. Aziz had on impulse invited the English ladies to undertake the expedition to the Marabar Hills, entirely ignorant of the Caves' history and nature. The Caves are, however, known to Professor Godbole and, one may assume, their mystery; but Aziz is unsuccessful in his attempt to get Godbole to describe them. His questions are met with polite evasion or silence:

> The comparatively simple mind of the Mohammedan was encountering Ancient Night. PI 80

The Brahman's conception of time and space would be unacceptable to the Mohammedan. Mrs. Moore thinks of Professor Godbole as she reels away from the Caves; Aziz, spiritually at home in a mosque, wishes to have Godbole with him to interpret the stark, primordial mystery of the Caves. The Brahman makes no conscious effort to bridge political or ethnic gaps, but he appears to have this effect. Even his dress is harmonious—

> as if he had reconciled the products of East and West, mental as well as physical, and could never be discomposed. PI 76

His song to Shri Krishna moves both Adela and Mrs. Moore profoundly. The god is invoked but he does not come. The guests and servants have listened enthralled. The silence that follows the song is piercingly beautiful.

Fielding who is so irritated by pettiness, ill-will, noise and suspicion in India, is nevertheless puzzled by Professor Godbole's being engulfed in tranquillity. Harmony is a prelude to silence, and it is this harmony Godbole seeks in the ritual celebrations at the birth of Krishna. This harmony embraces love of all men, the whole universe and 'the tiny splinters of detail'. It embraces Mrs. Moore and a wasp. Professor Godbole seems to contain the dissensions of race and creed. His mind works in a dimension incomprehensible to the Christians and Mohammedans, who from time to time are aware of his insight and would wish to share it to advance the frontiers of their own understanding. The submerged bridges and passages are built by Professor Godbole and, to a less extent, by Mrs. Moore. These two are linked together by the wasp, the caves and the Mau festival. Their minds at times overlap, although there is only one occasion, Fielding's tea-party, on which they meet. And each without being physically present has power to communicate with others. Fielding and Aziz are less susceptible to such communication, but Adela, at the time of her crisis, and Stella and Ralph tune in more readily.

Turtons and Burtons

In Chandrapore the Indians' collective name for the Anglo-Indians is the Turtons and Burtons. They think collectively of the English out of fear and hatred: the English act collectively in self-protection, which includes an element of fear and hatred. The English are constantly feeling the need to close the ranks, to toe the line, to teach quickly the newcomers what is pukka. Loyalty to the flag and submission to the local hierarchy must be unquestioned. An encrusted officialism results, in which every human relationship suffers. Ignorance of the arts is a positive virtue; individualism and imagination are handicaps in such an environment.

> ... the Arts were bad form, and Ronny had repressed his mother when she had enquired after his viola; a viola was almost a demerit, and certainly not the sort of instrument one mentioned in public.
>
> PI 43

Religion was bad form, too, if it meant more than endorsing the National Anthem. The Public School tradition flourished more strongly in India than England. A 'type' had been produced in England to become 'a good type' in India. Religion and the arts, where they demanded an individual response, destroyed 'the good type' and threatened the security of the herd.

The most frightening manifestation of herd feeling is at the times when the largest numbers are gathered together: at the

Bridge Party; at the club, to receive the martyred Heaslop and to ostracise the bounder, Fielding; and in the court. The women play a prominent part on all these occasions. At the Bridge Party the women, by claiming the attention of their menfolk, prevent them from meeting and talking to the Indians. Of the English-women, Mrs. Turton, the Collector's wife, is the only one on that occasion to speak to the Indian ladies, and then with a paralysing condescension. At the club, when Fielding senses the herd hysteria is generating an uncontrollable evil, and Major Callendar's exaggerated reports imply that Miss Quested's life is in danger,

> One young mother—a brainless but most beautiful girl—sat on a low ottoman in the smoking-room with her baby in her arms; her husband was away in the district, and she dared not return to her bungalow in case the 'niggers attacked'. The wife of a small railway official, she was generally snubbed; but this evening, with her abundant figure and masses of corn-gold hair, she symbolised all that is worth fighting and dying for; more permanent a symbol, perhaps, than poor Adela. 'Don't worry, Mrs. Blakiston, those drums are only Mohurram,' the men would tell her. 'Then they've started,' she moaned, clasping the infant and rather wishing he would not blow bubbles down his chin at such a moment as this. 'No, of course not, and anyhow, they're not coming to the club.' 'And they're not coming to the Burra Sahib's bungalow either, my dear, and that's where you and your baby'll sleep to-night,' answered Mrs. Turton, towering by her side like Pallas Athene, and determining in the future not to be such a snob.   PI 188–9

It is Mrs. Turton, too, who supports Major Callendar in his endeavour to disfigure, through surgery, Nawab Bahadur's grandson. In Callendar a racist's fear and hatred is shot through with a fierce sadism:

> 'His beauty's gone, five upper teeth, two lower and a nostril.... Old Panna Lal brought him the looking-glass yesterday and he blub-bered.... I laughed; I laughed, I tell you, and so would you; that used to be one of these buck niggers, I thought, now he's all septic; damn him, blast his soul—er—I believe he was unspeakably immoral—er—'   PI 225

Mrs. Turton's encouragement is 'At last some sense is being talked'. She it is, too, who when Adela withdraws her charge against Aziz in the court, pours on her a torrent of abuse. For the English she becomes the spearhead of racial domination. Their collective concern is not for justice but to achieve the utmost humiliation of the Indians. The rottenness of their cause on this occasion is emphasised by the stench in their homes.

> The Sweepers had just struck, and half the commodes of Chandra-pore remained desolate in consequence—   PI 223

The humiliation intended for the Indians rebounds on the English. McBryde's assessment of oriental pathology is given a sharp blow when his statement, that the darker races are physic-ally attracted by the fairer but not vice versa, is met by the anonymous interruption,

> 'Even when the lady is so uglier than the gentleman?'   PI 227

The second rebuff is delivered to the English when the magistrate insists on their climbing down from the platform, on to which they had trooped so ceremoniously. Their ultimate humiliation is Miss Quested's withdrawal of the charge. In the pandemonium that ensues the English escape out of the back of the court as best they can, but still endeavouring to preserve their collective identity. Miss Quested, however, is left behind by the Turtons and Burtons, and when she is swept by the triumphant crowd through the public exit towards the bazaars she encounters for the first time a fragment of the real India:

> . . . a tuft of scented cotton wool, wedged in an old man's ear . . .
>   PI 240

The Indians

The English are not alone in holding Bridge Parties. Some of the prominent Indians of Chandrapore form themselves into a committee 'where Hindus, Moslems, two Sikhs, two Parsis, a Jain, and a Native Christian tried to like one another more than came natural to them'. The success of such a gathering is no more than Turton's Bridge Party. The Indians' unity is achieved through abusing the English. Forster's prediction that such a committee would vanish if the English were to leave India has proved true. Neither English nor Indian groups have a constructive future if based on fear or hatred. Collectively the Indians are seen as unreliable, suspicious and childish. The paternal attitudes of the English have evoked from them a pattern of behaviour similar to that of rebellious adolescents. They are petulant, proud, defiant, but inordinately in need of kindness. Hamidullah, for instance, looks back nostalgically to the happy time he spent in Cambridge where personal relationships mattered more than the racial or political issues of nationalism.

> How happy he had been there, twenty years ago! Politics had not mattered in Mr. and Mrs. Bannister's rectory. There, games, work, and pleasant society had interwoven, and appeared to be sufficient substructure for a national life.   PI 111

It is, however, sadly ironic that Hamidullah, the most anglicised of the Indians, should be so brutal in his vindictiveness after the trial as to challenge Ronny about the details of his mother's death.

The passage between Indian and Indian is as obstructed as that between English and Indian. Forster questions fundamentally the concept of India as an entity. Fielding mocks Aziz's claim that India one day will be a nation, and Aziz himself knows in his heart that the gulf between Hindu and Moslem is too great for unity or nationhood to be achieved. One of the subtlest achievements of the novel is the author's success in conveying to the reader a sense of the unbridgeable gulf between Aziz, the Moslem, and Godbole, the Hindu. Both are highly educated Indians, working in close collaboration with the English, yet their religions and cultural backgrounds are so diverse, the roots of their being so distant, that they scarcely seem to breathe the same air. Aziz is by nature more poet than doctor; he is passionate, volatile, impulsive, with a craving for kindness and friendship. He is quick to sense injury and is not without vindictiveness. He has a love of beauty, a reverence for the past might of Islam, and

86

he cherishes hopes for a national unity in India, in which the power and beauty of Islam will once again be manifest. His openness, ability and apparent contempt for his English superior, Major Callendar, make him a ready target for the English.

Professor Godbole is an enigma. A heavy veil hangs between the Brahman's personality and its expression. For him there is no immediacy in time or space. The dimensions of his existence are different from Aziz's and Fielding's. As the guests are leaving after Fielding's tea-party, he stays them with a religious song. A most tiresome moment to choose to put himself in the position of a milkmaiden to sing to Shri Krishna, 'Come! come to me only'. This song, however, has a strange transforming influence on those who hear it and on the development of the story. Equally out of time is Godbole's bland request to Fielding, when the latter is desperately concerned about Aziz's arrest, that he should help in the naming of the new school at Mau. Should it be called Mr. Fielding High School or King-Emperor George the Fifth?

Aziz, on being met on the station at Chandrapore by the Police Inspector, impulsively tries to escape and then breaks down in despair. Godbole does not even acknowledge the situation as critical. He expounds on the shared responsibility for acts of good and evil, on the inter-relatedness of God's presence and His absence, and caps his deliberations with a story about a cow.

How, too, do their songs differ? Both occasions are marked by writing of the highest order. The quintessence of different Indian characteristics is distilled in these passages. Aziz recites his poem in his squalid bedroom with clusters of flies thick about the light; recalling the grandeur of the Islamic empire and giving the assurance that India is still one.

Godbole's song lacks the tenderness and pathos of Aziz's. It is not so clearly lodged in time or space. Shri Krishna is invoked but does not come, but his absence gives promise of his ultimate presence—a conception strange enough for Aziz, but entirely baffling for the occidental.

'But He comes in some other song, I hope?' said Mrs. Moore gently.

> 'Oh, no, he refuses to come,' repeated Godbole, perhaps not understanding her question. 'I say to Him, Come, come, come, come, come come. He neglects to come.'
>
> Ronny's steps had died away, and there was a moment of absolute silence. No ripple disturbed the water, no leaf stirred.   PI 84

Aziz's poem voices loneliness and isolation, and a yearning for friendship and past glory. Godbole's song is a plea for the god to appear. There is perfection in the silence that ensues. Forster reminds us that 'a perfectly adjusted organism would be silent'. In Aziz there is a bustle and restlessness which contrasts sharply with Godbole's impersonal calm and detachment. There seems little hope of any organism adjusting perfectly to a situation where Moslem must live cheek-by-jowl with a Hindu. The caves' discordant echo separates the English from the Indians; the collision of boats at the culmination of the Gokul Ashtami celebrations is a collision of cultures, all are capsized.

> They plunged into the warm shallow water, and rose struggling into a tornado of noise.   PI 328

Rapprochement

Akbar's mistake was that he invented a new religion that embraced the whole of India. Newcomers to India, such as Miss Quested, might hope for the fulfilment of this ideal, but even nationalists such as Aziz who yearn for such unity admit 'Nothing embraces the whole of India, nothing, nothing . . .'. Miss Quested instead of asking to see the real India might have fared better had she met the real Indian who would have comprised Aziz, Godbole, Ram Chand, Hamidullah, Mohammed Latif, the punkah-wallah in the court-room and a few dozen others. Men cannot be known by the institutions they represent: they can only be known and understood as individuals. In this respect Fielding's attitude, so different from his compatriots', is significant:

> Neither a missionary nor a student, he was happiest in the give-and-take of a private conversation. The world, he believed, is a globe of

men who are trying to reach one another and can best do so by the help of good will plus culture and intelligence—a creed ill suited to Chandrapore, but he had come out too late to lose it. He had no racial feeling—not because he was superior to his brother civilians, but because he had matured in a different atmosphere, where the herd-instinct does not flourish. The remark that did him most harm at the club was a silly aside to the effect that the so-called white races are really pinko-grey. He only said this to be cheery, he did not realise that 'white' has no more to do with a colour than 'God save the King' with a god, and that it is the height of impropriety to consider what it does connote. The pinko-grey male whom he addressed was subtly scandalised; his sense of insecurity was awoken, and he communicated it to the rest of the herd.   PI 65

Fielding's unprejudiced scrutiny of skin pigment is carried over into his teaching. He says

'I believe in teaching people to be individuals, and to understand other individuals. It's the only thing I do believe in. At Government College, I mix it up with trigonometry, and so on.'   PI 127

It is Fielding's support for Aziz and his belief in his innocence, without a scrap of supporting evidence, and in the face of his compatriots' herd antagonism, that vindicate his belief in personal relationships. But rapprochement on a personal basis will not solve India's political and ethnic problems. It is, however, the only approach, Forster considers, that has any efficacy.

'Mosque', 'Caves', and 'Temple' are the three sections of the book. They denote three critical encounters. In the first Aziz meets Mrs. Moore. His initial suspicion and sense of outrage are quickly swept aside by the respect she has shown in removing her shoes, by her belief that God is present in the mosque, and by her intuitive understanding of Aziz, for which he calls her an Oriental. East and West have met and formed a deep and lasting bond.

In the Marabar caves there is no real meeting, but a moment of hysteria followed by misunderstanding, recrimination and the ultimate separation of East and West. The caves are prehistoric; they predate Islam, Christianity and Hinduism.

89

To call them 'uncanny' suggests ghosts, and they are older than all spirit. Hinduism has scratched and plastered a few rocks, but the shrines are unfrequented, as if pilgrims, who generally seek the extraordinary, had here found too much of it.   PI 130

Mrs. Moore's experience of horror prepares us for Miss Quested's. Mrs. Moore's despair and subsequent lassitude derive from the sensation in the cave of smallness, insignificance. She feels she can no longer communicate with her children, Ralph and Stella; nor even with God. The caves which predate all communication of man or spirit have revealed to that withered priestess the pointlessness of the anxieties about bridges and passages, about ethnic differences. The echo has reduced everything to insignificance. The squabbles of English with Indian, or Moslem with Hindu, become derisory. She shows no interest whatsoever in Miss Quested's subsequent plight, but pays heed only when Adela refers to the echo.

In the 'Temple' the annual birth of Krishna is celebrated at the time of the monsoon. This Hindu ritual brings together on the one hand Fielding, Mrs. Moore's children by her second marriage, Ralph and Stella, and Aziz as spectators, and on the other Professor Godbole, as a Hindu celebrant. Ralph and Stella share their mother's priestly power. They see beyond things, and have an affinity with Hinduism without showing interest in its forms. When the boats collide with the floating image of the village of Gokul, all five are in the water. From this symbolic wetting English, Moslem and Hindu go their separate ways. Friendships have been formed, spiritual affinities sensed, but they part because neither mosque, nor cave, nor temple, nor the soil of India will contain them together. They have thrown into their relationships part of themselves, but it is not enough to keep them together. As the storm gathers the Hindus rush to the foreshore and prepare to throw God into the water. The analogue is inescapable:

Thus was He thrown year after year, and were others thrown— little images of Ganpati, baskets of ten-day corn, tiny tazias after Mohurram—scapegoats, husks, emblems of a passage; a passage not easy, not now, not here, not to be apprehended except when it is unattainable: the God to be thrown was an emblem of that.   PI 328

Forster completed his novel more than twenty years before the partition of India. His analysis of the possibilities of rapprochement was prophetic.

6

Critical Work

'ABINGER HARVEST'

This collection of articles, essays and reviews is arranged in four parts: The Present; Books; The Past; The East. Much of it sparkles, but there is dross too, especially when the author's enthusiasm for maiden aunts of moderate literary ability is the occasion for unwarrantable quotation. When Jane Austen is the maiden aunt the quotation and gloss are brilliant; when the maiden aunt is one of the four septuagenarian sisters of Hannah More, less pleasing.

With such minor exceptions this volume of essays is a joy to read because the author reveals himself and illuminates his subject with a frankness, gaiety and sweet reasonableness. The later novels are characterised by a complicated infolding of relationships. These essays are manifestly uncomplicated, brief, personal and invariably original. This originality is marked not so much by the author's acute perception as his angle of vision. He writes about Keats from the Abbeys' viewpoint, about Gibbon as a militia-man and about Coleridge under his alias of Trooper Silas Tomkyn Comberbacke.

Interesting autobiographical scraps abound. His attachment to Surrey is evinced in the local pageant. He buys his first property, a wood, with royalties earned in America by the popularity of *A Passage to India*. Forster's short story, 'Other Kingdom', written very many years earlier, is a sharp indictment of the acquisitive wood-owner, Harcourt Worters. Now, faced with the problem of a public foot-path running through his own wood, with children throwing stones or stealing the blackberries, with lovers flattening the bracken, Forster wryly sees himself as the

Selfish Giant type of landlord, preoccupied with fencing in his wood rather than enjoying it.

In these essays Forster frequently sees himself in ludicrous situations and laughs at his gaucheness with a quiet deprecation. His introduction to T. S. Eliot's poetry took place during the First World War. The circumstances are sufficiently unheroic to be Prufrockian:

> It was Egypt, no danger or discomfort; still it was the war, and while waiting for a tram in Cairo I sprained my ankle upon the asphalt pavement and was carried into the garden of a friend.
>
> AH 87

In this garden he reads the early poems of Eliot.

> ... they sang of private disgust and diffidence, and of people who seemed genuine because they were unattractive or weak. ... Here was a protest, and a feeble one, and the more congenial for being feeble. For what, in that world of gigantic horror, was tolerable except the slighter gestures of dissent?

Forster's eye for the slighter gestures turns on himself. He records his loutishness without false modesty. Our laughter is not without a deepening perception of the nature of strength and weakness. Howard Sturgis, the author of *Belchamber*, invited Forster to lunch.

> After lunch I made a little slip. My host led me up to the fireplace, to show me a finished specimen of his embroidery. Unluckily there were two fabrics near the fireplace, and my eye hesitated for an instant between them. There was a demi-semi-quaver of a pause. Then graciously did he indicate which his embroidery was, and then did I see that the rival fabric was a cloth kettle-holder, which could only have been mistaken for embroidery by a lout. Simultaneously I received the impression that my novels contained me rather than I them. He was very kind and courteous, but we did not meet again.
>
> AH 121

Forster's pose as the lout enables him from a humble position to highlight some of the idiosyncrasies in the more lofty. In 'Notes on the English Character' he maintains that the central flaw in the Englishman is an underdeveloped heart. It is not that the Englishman has no heart, but that since his public school days, when feeling was considered bad form, he had been inhibited from expressing great joy or sorrow. This tentativeness in the English character is caught in the early work of T. S. Eliot, which Forster so much admired.

The repression of feeling is at the heart of a number of Ibsen's plays. For instance the spring of tragedy in *Brand, Ghosts, Hedda Gabler, John Gabriel Borkman* and *The Masterbuilder* is the denial of love. Loftier or baser motives bring about this denial. In his essay on Ibsen, Forster looks for the source of Ibsen's poetic power, and finds it in the scenery of Norway, where the forces of nature may control the fortunes of men. Tonbridge, Cambridge, San Gimignano and India control the fortunes of Forster's characters. Places rather than natural scenery are the source of his inspiration. Ibsen and Wordsworth look beyond man-made places.

> At some date previous to his Italian journey he must have had experiences of passionate intensity among the mountains, comparable to the early experiences of Wordsworth in the English lakes ... they were both of them haunted until the end of their lives by the romantic possibilities of scenery.   AH 85

The analogy with Wordsworth is at first disquieting, but for Ibsen and Wordsworth this early and intense experience had caused both men to lead their thoughts and characters away from towns and cities, away even from houses or huts, to the freedom of water, ice and mountain.

'Mr. and Mrs. Abbey's Difficulties' is a piece of biographical research. It is an example of the denial of love in the name of duty. The Abbeys are entrusted with a large sum of money which is left for the bringing up of four children: John, George, Tom and Fanny. The boys are provided for parsimoniously; Fanny is prevented from corresponding with, or visiting them, even when one is on the point of death. The Abbeys are respectable business people. They have invested the money, and the interest accrues cosily, while George emigrates to America, Tom and John die of consumption, and Fanny elopes from their home in the arms of a Spaniard.

Forster gives us here the Abbeys' view of the Keats children, but in his coyness does not reveal the surname until the end. Out of duty the Abbeys kept their wards ignorant of the fortune that was to come to them.

> Tom and John remained ignorant until the day of their death, while Fanny believed for many years that she was a pauper and owed Mrs. Abbey for her board and lodgings. Much extravagance was averted by this timely reticence, many loans to undesirable friends, and tours both in England and on the Continent, which could have led to no useful purposes.   AH 231

Oddly enough the sum left for the children was £8,000. The same amount was left Forster by his great-aunt nearly a hundred years later. He was then in a position to tour England, the Continent and beyond. This essay, juxtaposing John Keats's tender but frustrated concern for his sister with the Abbeys' addiction to a code of duty which obliterates personal affections, is a controlled but bitter indictment of the underdeveloped heart.

Irony's finest stroke is so deft a decapitation that the reader is in some doubt as to whether the head has been severed at all. R. W. Chapman's 1923 edition of Jane Austen's novels and his 1932 edition of her letters are treated by Forster with full solemnity. Chapman is praised for his erudition, attention to detail, emendations and annotations; to say nothing of his illustrations. These

> are beyond all praise. Selected from contemporary prints, from fashion plates, manuals of dancing and gardening, tradesmen's advertisements, views, plans, etc., they have the most wonderful power of stimulating the reader . . .   AH 146

In the most courteous and civilised manner Chapman is demolished. The pedantry 'in his disquisitions on punctuation and travel, his indexes', his misreading of *Sanditon*, and the deficient judgment that leads him to find the triviality of the letters delightful, are mocked with the finest irony. Forster asks what would Jane Austen have thought of these volumes. His review

implies what she might have thought of R. W. Chapman and his
eight indexes,

> ... one of which distinguishes the various generations of the
> Austen family by four types of print—namely *AUSTEN*, AUSTEN,
> Austen, and *Austen*.   AH 154

His treatment of R. W. Chapman's edition of Jane Austen's
works is at some length, because he prizes highly this author's
mastery of style, delicacy of taste, and the finesse of her irony. Her
editor has not been so perceptive. But it is characteristic of
Forster's generosity as a critic that the endeavour of these three
essays is to shed light on Jane Austen's work rather than heave
more bric-à-brac at the severed head of the misguided editor.

'ASPECTS OF THE NOVEL'

Forster was invited to give the 1927 Clark lectures under the
auspices of Trinity College, Cambridge. The Clark lectures were
open to all members of the University, and invariably the lecturer
invited was a distinguished man of letters. The lecturer in 1926
had been T. S. Eliot. I believe Forster accepted the invitation with
no great zest. It put him in the position of being considered and
criticised as a scholar; a dubious honour: literary criticism of this
extended kind demanded a certain amount of systematisation
and generalisation—uncongenial tasks for Forster. Furthermore
his modesty permitted him to think of himself as no more than a
pseudo-scholar; his honesty led him to assure his audience that
they too were in no higher category. As a work of scholarship,
therefore, this volume is no heavyweight. As a light to the reader
of novels it is brilliant. The lectures are devoid of fuss or pretension. They are lucid, witty, generous and above all illuminating.
Forster's great gift as a critic is his freshness of vision. He has no
truck with the second-hand. He has no need, because his own
excitement at rediscovering the treasure of Dostoevsky or Jane
Austen or Melville brims over. The novelists have seized our
imaginations and whisked us off into their different worlds.
Forster alerts us to the craft and cunning of the transport.

One of the misgivings Forster might have had about these

lectures was his belief that at best the critic is a poor sort of creature, anatomising rather pathetically. In considering the contribution to the novel of poetry, religion and passion, he writes,

> ... we have not placed them yet, and since we are critics—only critics—we must try to place them, to catalogue the rainbow.

AN 137

He certainly scolds the novelist who, within a work of art, changes his viewpoint from creator to critic. Fielding and Thackeray are guilty of this, when they take the reader into their confidence about their characters.

> It is confidences about the individual people that do harm, and beckon the reader away from the people to an examination of the novelist's mind. Not much is ever found in it at such a moment, for it is never in the creative state: the mere process of saying 'come along, let's have a chat' has cooled it down. AN 112

Although fully aware of the folly of 'cataloguing the rainbow', Forster realises the need of some sort of systematisation within the lectures. He is averse to propounding critical theories and then lining up his novelists to do these theories service. The chronological approach he rejects after having paired off analogous passages from authors hundreds of years apart. He argues against an approach to his subject through the development of the novel, acknowledging the partial truth of 'History develops, Art stands still'. Classification by subject-matter he thinks even sillier. In his anxiety to escape from the principles, systems and apparatus of criticism he chooses the title *Aspects* 'because it is unscientific and vague'. These aspects are: The Story; People; The Plot; Fantasy and Prophecy; Pattern and Rhythm. It is of interest to compare these aspects with Aristotle's six parts of tragedy: plot; character; diction; thought; spectacle; song. And it comes as no surprise that within these Clark lectures Aristotle is frequently invoked.

Although Forster looked to Aristotle for guidance in arriving at the format of his lectures, he parted company with him when it came to botanising and anatomising art-forms. Aristotle had a professional interest in such activities; Forster remained sceptical of systems or simplifications.

> All simplifications are fascinating, all lead away from truth (which lies nearer the muddle of Tristram Shandy)...   AN 158

Aristotle took the business of criticism very solemnly; Forster, confessing himself a pseudo-scholar, warns his audience of the limitations of such a business. It may help another pseudo-scholar to pass his examination without advancing his education a jot. In this sense

> A paper on 'King Lear' may lead somewhere, unlike the rather far-fetched play of the same name.

Where does the novel as a work of art lead to? Forster would say, to enjoyment, to a stirring of our imagination and a sharpening of our discriminatory faculties, to a finer appreciation of moral concern or prophetic power, and to the aesthetic delight at the craftsman's accomplishment when manner and matter are happily married.

The pursuit of excellence in this field of literature leads us past the English novelists to the French and the Russian. There is a greater glow about the writing when we read of Proust's mastery of rhythm in threading the little phrase of Vinteuil through his great work; when a passage from Dostoevsky's *The Brothers Karamazov* is compared with a passage from George Eliot's *Adam Bede*; or when Forster describes how Tolstoy's sense of space, part of his 'divine equipment', manifests itself in *War and Peace*.

On the other hand there is no need to don a national hair-shirt for the frailty of the English novel. In any case Forster is never given to mournful breast-beating. He himself has derived infinite pleasure from his reading of the English novel, and he clearly sees it as one of his tasks to convey something of that pleasure through these lectures. At times this pleasure is not without qualification. Wells and Dickens he admires for their inventiveness and energy, but thinks they had no sense of beauty. Scott's ability to tell a story is admitted, but this is an ability

Forster does not prize highly. This ability helped Scheherazade to avoid her fate. It also kept Neanderthal man gaping over his camp-fire. Forster has little sympathy with authors who rely on suspense to keep the reader awake. He praises Scott's story-telling skill, but deplores his lack of artistic detachment and passion.

Passion, too, he finds lacking in Henry James. He is at pains to be generous in his assessment of James, because he is all too aware of a fundamental difference of temper between himself and James. In the lecture on 'Pattern and Rhythm' he illustrates very fully James's concern for a form that is aesthetically pleasing. In this endeavour, James in *The Ambassadors*, Forster concedes, is entirely successful, but the price that has to be paid

> is that most of human life has to disappear before he can do us a novel.

His characters are few in number, and they are mostly drained of vitality.

> They are incapable of fun, of rapid motion, of carnality, and of nine-tenths of heroism. Their clothes will not take off . . . AN 205

When discussing character Forster is at his most penetrating. His division between flat and round characters is a facile convenience, and because it is a generalisation it is subject to many exceptions; but this definition is the occasion for an illuminating detail from *Mansfield Park*. Forster shows how Jane Austen, by a delicate adjustment of the dialogue, can change Lady Bertram from a flat to a round character and back again, and such a change, or rather a glimpse of Lady Bertram's extended life, is for a deeply felt moral purpose. In the depiction of Jane Austen's characters there is fun, artistry and moral fervour. There is little enough fun when the prophet-novelists forge their work.

Dostoevsky, Melville, D. H. Lawrence and Emily Brontë are the only novelists, Forster believes, who can illustrate his theme of prophecy. 'Prophetic fiction', he maintains,

> . . . demands humility and the absence of the sense of humour. It reaches back. . . . It is spasmodically realistic. And it gives us the sensation of a song or of sound. AN 176

These are the novelists with poetry and passion. Hardy, although a philosopher and a great poet, is excluded. His novels, in Forster's view, 'are surveys, they do not give out sounds . . . the characters do not reach back'. Conrad, who like Hardy has a poetic and emotional philosophy, reflects on life and things. In Forster's definition a prophet does not reflect. I believe there are many readers of Hardy and Conrad who fail to see the logic of Forster's exclusion of them from the prophetic band. On the other hand he is at pains to distinguish between D. H. Lawrence the preacher, whom he rejects, and D. H. Lawrence, the prophet, 'who has the rapt bardic quality, and whom it is idle to criticise'.

Melville, too, has the bardic quality, but the words are more difficult to catch.

> The essential in 'Moby Dick', its prophetic song, flows athwart the action and the surface morality like an undercurrent. It lies outside words. AN 179

Forster attributes the mystery of Melville's prophetic song to the author's conception of evil. In this is Melville's strength which sets his work soaring. *Billy Budd*, another of Melville's studies of evil, Forster calls 'a song not without words'. In 1950 Forster was to find his own words for that song, when in close collaboration with Benjamin Britten he wrote the libretto for the now world-famous opera. In Melville, as in the other prophet-novelists, Forster acknowledges the song, the reaching back to what, in Jungian phraseology, would be called the archetypal pattern, and the extraordinary gift of describing particular things and events but focusing on the universal.

The lectures end with the striking prophecy that although

> we may harness the atom, we may land on the moon, we may abolish or intensify warfare, the mental processes of animals may be understood,

the novelist of the future will still have to rely on his creative faculty to assimilate, select and describe these new facts of history and their effect, if any, on human nature.

The essays, articles and broadcasts in this volume were mostly composed between 1936 and 1951. They are presented in two sections: Part I entitled 'The Second Darkness' deals essentially with political issues; Forster writes under the cloud of war which began, for Britain, in 1939 and which he thought of as still going on in 1951; and in that sense, the situation is unchanged in 1969. Part II is entitled 'What I Believe' and is about the arts on the one hand, and places on the other. A characteristic of this volume is that political arguments are frequently illuminated by reference to the arts, and evaluation of the arts might rest on political criteria. For instance, at the 1937 Paris Exhibition Forster sees among Van Gogh's paintings his 'Potato-eaters':

> Here are pictures of potatoes and of miners who have eaten potatoes until their faces are tuberous and dented and their skins grimed and unpeeled. They are hopeless and humble, so he loves them.   TC 16

He compares it with Picasso's 'Guernica', a memorial to the savage bombing of an undefended Spanish town:

> The fresco is indignant, and so it is less disquieting than the potato-feeders of Van Gogh. Picasso is grotesquely angry, and those who are angry still hope.   TC 17

Both artists, in their work, are concerned with suffering. It is characteristic of Forster to prefer the less rhetorical.

The substance of his argument in the essay 'Does Culture Matter?' (1940) is that in the midst of war a country needs to be alerted to the traditions and culture it is fighting for. There is a danger that the artists might disappear from a state-organised society and that 'culture will be jettisoned'. Forster is anxious that we should salvage not just books, paintings and music, but also the power to enjoy them. His anxiety that we should stand fast against fascism, against vulgarisation of taste, and not let go those things we hold as priceless and unique, leads him to speak with an unwonted fervour. He is no longer secretive, playing guessing games as in the *Abinger Harvest* essay about the Abbeys. There is no delicate irony when he speaks of anti-semitism or the Nazi ideals. Unblushingly as a patriot he aligns himself with Milton, on the tercentenary of the publication of the 'Areopagitica', and calls for us to reject the tyranny abroad and to guard jealously our liberty at home. But for our democracy he gives only two cheers:

> one because it admits variety and two because it permits criticism.
> TC 79

Within this collection there are three essays about music: 'The C Minor of that Life'; 'Not Listening to Music'; 'George Crabbe and Peter Grimes'. There is also a handsome tribute to Bernard Shaw as music critic in 'The Raison d'Etre of Criticism in the Arts'. Through these essays one hears directly, what one gathers only piecemeal through the novels, the considerable impact music made on Forster's life. Lucy's playing of Beethoven in *A Room with a View*, the visit to the opera in *Where Angels Fear to Tread*, the goblins of Beethoven's Fifth Symphony that prance through *Howards End*, Ronny's suppression of his viola and the haunting song of Professor Godbole in *A Passage to India*, are not incidental elements in the novels, but of integral importance.

In *Abinger Harvest*, *Aspects of the Novel* and *Two Cheers for Democracy* Forster examines Marcel Proust's *A la Recherche du Temps Perdu*. He is fascinated by nothing so much in this vast work as the little phrase in the music of Vinteuil, which threads its way through the novel, recalling and refining an emotional response in the reader. On a different scale with different effect Forster introduces Godbole's song and its echoes in *A Passage to India*.

Forster's friendship and collaboration with Benjamin Britten has been one of the most joyous experiences of his long life. He was fascinated by Crabbe's hatred of Aldeburgh, yet his inability to write effective poetry of any other setting. Britten's music for the opera *Peter Grimes* affects Forster deeply. This opera was the genesis of the Aldeburgh Festival to which at a later date Britten and Forster were to contribute *Billy Budd*.

Two essays appear next to each other in the middle of the

book: 'Three Stories by Tolstoy' and 'Edward Carpenter'. Forster is interested in both authors because neither was happy with the class into which he was born, and both wanted to live and work with manual labourers. Tolstoy, despite his own complexity, believed in simplicity: Forster illustrates how this belief showed its different facets at various periods in Tolstoy's life. Carpenter, forsaking his middle-class background, went to live in Sheffield, befriending artisans, the unemployed, and toughs, keeping his private income of five hundred a year, and trying to be a socialist. These essays reveal something of Forster's sympathies. He was entirely without pretension. What he wrote of Carpenter was partly true of himself.

> As he had looked outside his own class for companionship, so he was obliged to look outside his own race for wisdom.　　　TC 219

Although never a manual worker, Forster was more at ease when there was no call to fuss about his appearance. John Arlott, in an essay on 'Forster and Broadcasting' from *Aspects of E. M. Forster*, mentions his preferring, when he was in India, the company of Indians to that of English people, and that he usually travelled second class on trains so that he could mix happily with the Indians. On his winter visits to the broadcasting studio he would appear 'in a long, rather worn overcoat, and a heavy woollen scarf, carefully safety-pinned across his chest and not to be removed, even in a centrally-heated studio'.

Tolstoy's stages of simplicity, as exemplified in three stories, are libido, placidity and saintliness. Less complicated than Tolstoy, and free from the ravages of introspection and remorse, Forster's belief in simplicity rests more on moral and intellectual honesty. The essay ends with the question 'how do you think simplicity can be worked in a world that has become industrialised?' It is one of the questions that haunts *Howards End* as the red rust of London creeps outwards.

Simplicity of expression marks Forster's writing. *Two Cheers for Democracy* contains no less than sixteen articles which were originally broadcast, and their success depended on lucidity of style and the modesty of their delivery. The lucidity is the achievement of an old professional, the delivery seemingly straightforward but, in its control and effect, subtly attuned to the medium.

These broadcasts reached millions of ears, in England and India. The outbreak of the Second World War spurred Forster to speak out unequivocally against totalitarianism, although he was fully aware that to crush such a system called for a temporary build-up of a similar structure. For this reason he alerted us to the defence of civil liberties and to the defence of the freedoms enjoyed in a democracy. He was, nevertheless, not deluded into thinking that a political solution was the panacea of the world's ills. This had not been the solution for India. It was not for the world. Three cheers are merited not by democracy, but by Love, the Beloved Republic.

What does he mean by love? In the Prefatory Note he says

> though we cannot expect to love one another, we must learn to put up with one another. Otherwise we shall all of us perish.

Is he then advocating no more than tolerance as the solution for survival? He certainly despairs of love in the public or international sector. 'Love in public affairs does not work', and he deplores the attempts of those who try to foster good will by arranging international sporting events. Such events, in Forster's view, help 'to kick the world downhill'. On a personal basis, he maintains, it is fatuous to try to love people one does not like. Ansell's advice to Rickie in *The Longest Journey* was

> 'If you don't like people, put up with them as well as you can. Don't try to love them: you can't, you'll only strain yourself.'

Tolerance, he admits, is a dull virtue but

> 'This is the only force which will enable different races and classes and interests to settle down together to the work of reconstruction.'
>
> TC 56

Auden claims Forster's allegiance when he writes 'We must love one another or die'. In Forster's interpretation of 'The Enchafèd Flood' we see a little of what is meant by that 'love'. It calls for a new heroism, for men to work together to build a new city. The days of the heroic nomad are past, the Beloved Republic has yet to be born.

> Auden's hope—reinforced in his case by Christian dogma—is the world's hope and its only hope. For some of us who are non-Christian there still remains the comfort of the non-human, the relief, when we look up at the stars, of realising that they are uninhabitable. But not there for any of us lies our work or our home.   TC 276

7

Biography

Forster has written no autobiography. His elusiveness has lessened with the years; his modesty has remained. To have a camera directed at him has always been an embarrassment.

> When a camera approaches he looks at it, it looks at him, and they have nothing to say to each other. He produces an official silence, the camera produces an unlikeness. ASPECTS OF E. M. FORSTER, p. 62

To draw attention to himself as the central figure for the public's consideration would be alien both to his art and his nature. But he has written three biographies, each of which has autobiographical material. This is Forster's way of writing about himself and the things he cherishes. In his essays and lectures he has declared himself politically, culturally and, to an extent, personally. His personal affections, for example, shine through his references to T. E. Lawrence and his visits to Clouds Hill. Later in his life his association with Benjamin Britten and Aldeburgh was a further enrichment. He links his friends with the places they live in. When he thinks of his family he thinks, too, of the places they have lived in: his mother's home in Hertfordshire, the model for Howards End; Abinger Hammer; and, above all, Battersea Rise.

Battersea Rise, the home of the Thorntons, represented to Forster his heritage of class and wealth. He looks back on this inheritance with a mixture of pride and guilt. It lacked love; it lacked spirit. Love he found in his mother's family, the Whichelos; the spiritual life opened up for him at Cambridge. His experiences in India were to deepen his spiritual perception, and to lead him to champion love as the only salvation of mankind.

In writing biographically of Marianne Thornton, Goldsworthy Lowes Dickinson, and the Maharajah of Dewas State Senior, Forster has revealed the three most formative influences in his own life: his family; Cambridge; India.

'GOLDSWORTHY LOWES DICKINSON'

Why did Forster write this biography? Was it because he had known Goldie for thirty-five years and had known him well for twenty? Forster was not blind to Dickinson's shortcomings as a letter-writer, poet, pamphleteer, essayist and novelist. At times the praise seems scarcely justified, and at times minor works obtrude. Forster admits that the writers who meant most to Dickinson: Shelley, Plato and Goethe, held no particular appeal for him. Dickinson, however, had shown himself a tried and affectionate friend, and represented for Forster the spirit of independence, tolerance and progressive thought, so treasured at King's College, Cambridge. Dickinson was eminent as a teacher, but it was to Nathaniel Wedd rather than to Dickinson that Forster himself felt more deeply indebted:

> When I was at King's, Wedd taught me classics and it is to him rather than to Dickinson—indeed to him more than to anyone—that I owe such awakening as has befallen me. GLD 73

Through taking Dickinson as his subject, rather than Wedd, Forster could cover not only a greater span of Cambridge life, but also a much broader field of contemporary politics and arts. It gave him scope to include the Cambridge Apostles, the Bloomsbury set, and to give the background to his own political thinking, 'the fag-end of Victorian liberalism'.

Dickinson was sixteen years older than Forster, but as their friendship developed they discovered that they shared many interests. Music was precious to them both, and strengthened in them a conviction of transcendental truth. Their liking for Mozart, Wagner and Beethoven was more in accord than their literary taste, but they were both prepared to defend their culture against the Marxian philosophy of art, on the same grounds.

Art, literature, music, culture are not external decorations, but age-long secretions in the soul of man, and one of the problems of our revolution is to prevent man from despising or forgetting his own past. Thus although he [Dickinson] came more and more to condemn our economic system and advocate drastic changes, he had no sympathy whatever with the Marxian who rejects Shakespeare and Tchekov on the ground that they wrote for Capitalists.   GLD 88

In *Two Cheers for Democracy* Forster returns repeatedly to this theme. The onrush of war, with its consequent brutalisation, filled him with a sense of urgency to fight a rear-guard action for the supremacy of art.

The work of art stands up by itself, and nothing else does. It achieves something which has often been promised by society, but always delusively. Ancient Athens made a mess—but the 'Antigone' stands up. Renaissance Rome made a mess—but the ceiling of the Sistine got painted . . .   TC 101

Dickinson and Forster were patriots, not in the sense that, when England was at war, they felt impelled to jump into a uniform, seize a rifle, and fight; but that they felt duty-bound to reassert traditional values and national virtues, and to be about the business of building the peace in the midst of war. Dickinson was an architect of the League of Nations, during the First World War; Forster's broadcasts during the Second World War were extraordinarily impressive, and, in retrospect, no less effective. They were patriots, too, in the sense that they knew well, in physical terms, the country they loved. They were both great walkers, and the character of England unfolded itself to them on their walking holidays, as it never can to the modern motorist. Above all, it was King's College, Cambridge, that brought them together, and it was there they were to meet, off and on, during their thirty-five years' friendship.

Dickinson and Forster both came to Cambridge after a wretchedly unhappy time at public school. Their admission to King's was as balm. This part of the biography glows with a love for King's, because the author, no less than his subject, had a debt to record to the College and the University which gave him scope for happiness and fulfilment. Cambridge was for friendship, philosophy and talk. Dickinson mistrusted research as much as Forster mistrusted 'study' or 'criticism', which he nearly always found irrelevant. As learning becomes more closely associated with breadwinning, Dickinson voices his dismay:

> 'The spectacle of learning gets more depressing to me every year ... I care only for fruitful and vital handling of the eternal commonplaces or else for a new insight that will really help some one to internal freedom.'
> GLD 104

His reputation as a teacher was higher; his accessibility and friendliness to undergraduates marked the importance he attributed to the personal influence that promotes learning. Forster gives an example:

> I remember watching a perky undergraduate ferreting about in his books and him saying to me gently 'I don't know his name—he calls me Goldie'.
> GLD 197

There were many more, as perky, undergraduates to follow, who were in similar circumstances, to call the most distinguished Fellow of King's, 'Morgan'.

In 1912 Dickinson, R. C. Trevelyan and Forster travelled together to India. Dickinson was a tireless tourist, lecturing to a wide variety of audiences. He moved on from India to China and Japan, despairing of India's future:

> '... everything in India will have to be and ought to be swept away ...'
> GLD 149

Whereas he predicted a great future for the Chinese, he considered India had only a past. Forster agreed wholeheartedly with his indictment of Anglo-Indian society,

> 'It's the women more than the men that are at fault. There they are, without their children, with no duties, no charities, with empty minds and hearts, trying to fill them by playing tennis and despising the natives ...'
> GLD 141

but differed radically from Dickinson's view that there could be no rapprochement between the English and the Indians, simply 'because the Indians bore the English'. Forster suggests that Dickinson, in making such a statement, was overtired, and regrets that

> he never found in Indian society either the happiness or the peacefulness which have made my own visits to the country so wonderful.
>
> GLD 141

Forster's next essay in biography testifies to that peace and happiness.

'THE HILL OF DEVI'

This work, published in 1953, is a biography in the sense that its central concern is with the life and death of the Maharajah of Dewas State Senior. It comprises a collection of carefully edited letters written from India in 1912–13 and 1921, and additional passages about the 'State and its Ruler' and the 'Catastrophe'. The letters were addressed to the author's mother and other relatives. This brief but extraordinary document affirms that Forster, at least, was not bored by Indians, and that he looked on his time spent in Dewas as the ruler's private secretary as the great opportunity of his life.

The catastrophe that befalls Dewas State Senior is bankruptcy, followed by the humiliation and death of the Maharajah. This takes place in 1937, sixteen years after Forster's last visit to Dewas, but evidence of such impending fate abounded in the muddled administration he encountered when he took up his post as H.H. Private Secretary in 1921. When Forster's greatest Indian friend, Ross Masood, visited Dewas, he left after three days, distressed at this extreme example of his country's incompetence. On one occasion he and Forster were sent up Devi on an elephant on which the howdah had not been properly fixed. Their journey was made even less secure by the elephant continually covering his head with spray. On another, they were taken to Gwalior to a tea-party of saddhus, covered in different coloured ash, sitting on spikes.

Forster could tolerate muddle, more than Masood, especially if it sprang from affection; and in Dewas Senior he met deep and lasting affection and an irrepressible boyish jollity. He describes how, on April Fool's Day, various traps are set for him by the Maharajah:

> He sent me a message to my office asking me to go at once to a remote shed in the garden since something peculiar had been observed there. I excused myself. Nor, when bidden to refreshment, did I accept a cigarette of unusual shape. Nor was I asked to get an electric shock by sitting on a sofa. But I did drink some whisky-and-salt, to the court's uncategorical delight. Foolery, fun, practical jokes, bawdry—I was to be involved in them all as soon as I felt myself safe. He even made a pun on my name which eludes quotation: too indecent, too silly. But gay, gay. HD 62

Gaiety is in the middle of the most appalling muddle of the Gokul Ashtami festival. As the cymbals clash, the several choirs sing, the bands play—'Nights of Gladness' is part of their repertoire—Forster, to spare the Maharajah's feelings, buries the ill-fated ornamental fish in a flower pot. Tired and deafened to a state bordering on collapse, he sees the festival through to the end, carrying his painted stick, being fed with milk-soaked grain, having butter daubed on his forehead, and smothered in red and black powder. The allure of a lady fanatic, however, does not escape him, and he refers to her in a similar way in *A Passage to India:*

> She was gaudily yet neatly dressed in purple and yellow, a circlet of jasmine flowers was round her chignon and in her hands were a pair of tongs with which she accompanied herself. We could not discover whether she was praising God with or without attributes. Her voice was too loud. She nodded and smiled in a very pleasant way. HD 111

Forster's novel about India derives essentially from the impact of his two visits to the country. His letters record the affection, friendship, muddle and great beauty he found there. They also record a few vivid experiences, such as the Gokul Ashtami festival, which accrued a significance in the novel over and above that which it is afforded in *The Hill of Devi*. A further example is the accident in which an unidentified animal charged at a car carrying visitors to Dewas. The Maharajah is concerned to know what sort of animal it was, and he recalls that years ago he ran over a man on the same spot.

> 'I was not at all to blame—he was drunk and ran on to the road and I was cleared at the enquiry, and I gave money to his family. But ever since then he has been trying to kill me in the form you describe.' HD 90

It is the same shadow that haunts the Nawab Bahadur in *A Passage to India*.

Muddle, pride, childishness, bring about the Maharajah's downfall. The Government reorganise his children's future, his exchequer and his state. It seems he was bent on his own destruction and even the good offices of tried and trusted English friends were of no avail. The British Government, Forster says, were impeccably right and absolutely wrong. A failure of imagination is implied. *The Times* obituary similarly concerns itself with concentrating on the administrative weaknesses of a self-indulgent Indian Prince. Forster published *The Hill of Devi* as a tribute to this Prince and to his religion which 'was the deepest thing in him'. It is a testament of friendship.

'MARIANNE THORNTON'

Marianne Thornton was Forster's great-aunt. She lived from 1797 to 1887. The biography is in four parts: daughter; sister; aunt; great-aunt. The Thorntons were of evangelical Yorkshire stock, graduating from trade to banking. Battersea Rise, Marianne's home for the best part of a century, was bought by her father in 1792. He trebled its size with extensions and 'improvements', and built two other houses of similar style close by, and rented them to his friends. For nearly a hundred years Battersea Rise was the home of a very large and very wealthy English family. The period begins with the daughter, Marianne, hearing from Hannah More, a close friend of the family, about the literary set with whom she passed her youth: Johnson;

Burke; Horace Walpole; Mrs. Montagu; and ends with the great-aunt encouraging her recalcitrant great-nephew to raise a cheer for Queen Victoria on the occasion of her Golden Jubilee. It is strange that the longevity of this family is such that the lives of the great-aunt and great-nephew span nearly two hundred years. The great-aunt was born in the year *Pride and Prejudice* was written; the great-nephew's ninetieth birthday was celebrated, a few days after the first astronauts had orbited the moon, by a concert at King's College, Cambridge, by a volume entitled *Aspects of E. M. Forster*, which comprises essays and recollections by friends, and by a tea-party in his honour held by the Cambridge Humanists. In the first eight years of his life Great-aunt Marianne and his mother referred to him as 'the Important One'. There is a gay irony in this assessment.

This work is subtitled 'A Domestic Biography' and, rather than reflecting the changing literary tastes of the 19th century, deals with the family involvement in banking, education, house-keeping, family prayers and family politics. Indeed, if the Thorntons had had better literary taste, the biography might have been more engaging. The great-nephew's first encounter with the *Swiss Family Robinson* is exciting reading compared with the list of groceries purchased for a children's Christmas party in 1885. The Thorntons stood firmly for prose not passion. Their wealth had been acquired through common sense and diligence, they added to it by exercising the same qualities. They were liberal to the extent of supporting Wilberforce wholeheartedly in his work to abolish the slave trade; but their attitude to education for the working classes was motivated solely by the thought that better servants might thereby be available for the upper middle classes.

From the tenderest years it had been instilled into Marianne that she should impart her knowledge to the less fortunate. It was a common sight for the family carriage to stop by a group of poor people, and for the pious occupants to get out, teach the deferential ignorant, and drive on. This was part of Marianne's routine as a child. In later life she devoted herself on the one hand to the education of her twenty nieces and nephews, some of whom she took to the Continent, and on the other to promoting education in the elementary schools. She was moved by her dislike of ignorance and her 18th-century faith in reason, but she firmly believed that if children of the lower classes knew more, they would grow up happier, healthier and more helpful in service. With the latter in mind she applauded the achievement of Whitelands, an institution for training 'humble unpretending Village Teachers, making them clean and cook and iron (not wash) that they mayn't fancy themselves fine ladies *because* they teach them Geography and History and so on'.

These trainee teachers must not give themselves airs, they must know their place; but they are by no means in the most menial category. They should not be expected to *wash*. A nice appreciation of class differences is frequently evident in Forster's work. He recounts within this biography the family crisis over his Aunt Maimie marrying Mr. Aylward, a respectable middle-class Salisbury citizen with a keen and cultured interest in music. Maimie's brother 'had felt obliged to resign his Salisbury curacy when the scandal started, and neither the Close nor the County could call on her or go beyond bowing at bazaars, because she was Trade'.

For the young Forster and his mother Battersea Rise was grand but oppressive. Aunt Marianne's appetite for youth was cannibalistic. Mother and son were glad to return to their Hertford-shire home which was to exert an atavistic influence on the author's life:

> It certainly was a lovable little house, and still is, though it now stands just outside a twentieth-century hub and almost within sound of a twentieth-century hum. The garden, the overhanging wych-elm, the sloping meadow, the great view to the west, the cliff of fir trees to the north, the adjacent farm through the high tangled hedge of wild roses were all utilised by me in *Howards End*, and the interior is in the novel too. . . . From the time I entered the house at the age of four . . . I took it to my heart and hoped, as Marianne had of Battersea Rise, that I should live and die there.   MT 269

In Hertfordshire the 'Important One' was lonely, apart from the occasional companionship of young farm-hands or gardener's boy. Ansell, as mentioned earlier, was his regular Wednesday afternoon playfellow. Forster remembers him with deep affection. It is perhaps one of the reasons why Forster has been unhesitatingly classless in his friendships.

He was destined to leave his beloved Hertfordshire home as Marianne had to leave Battersea Rise. Her brother had married his deceased wife's sister, Emily. The family had been outraged. After a long period abroad Henry Thornton and his wife returned to Battersea Rise and Marianne and her ménage had to move to a house on Clapham Common. A week before she died she wrote to Emily Thornton asking for some milk, and it was sent her. Forster's inference is that she wished, before death came, to be in physical touch with Battersea Rise. 'The milk was a sacrament.'

In her will she left to her great-nephew sufficient money, the interest on which covered his school and university education, and two years of foreign travel. At twenty-five he inherited the capital. By this time his vocation as a writer was settled, and he was on his way to becoming the Important One to a circle wider than his family.

8

Achievement

> The truth is, of course, that you are a very great writer . . . my book stinks of me: whereas yours is universal.

This is T. E. Lawrence's tribute to Forster. He is comparing his own work *Seven Pillars of Wisdom* with *A Passage to India*. T. E. Lawrence was not a critic, but his assessment of Forster's work, contained in his letters, shows as deep an understanding of Forster's genius as any of the professional critics. Lawrence was not unqualified to recognise greatness in men and in literature. Forster, who was so shy of the critic, whose work he found almost invariably irrelevant, would be pleased to be remembered in the letters of a friend, for whom he had a deep respect and affection. Indeed, his greatest achievement might not be the literature he has left us but the friendships he has made—with the great and the insignificant. His belief in personal relations has been even more vividly exemplified in his life than in his writing.

In this last chapter we shall hear a little of what both friends and critics have said of Forster. Although he has five famous novels to his credit, many have thought that after the publication of *A Passage to India* in 1924 he dried up. Two novels are unpublished, one an early work referred to by Rose Macaulay, and the other a deeply personal work, which in 1927 he gave T. E. Lawrence to read.

> I wanted to read your long novel, and was afraid to. It was like your last keep, I felt: and if I read it I had you: and supposing I hadn't liked it? I'm so funnily made up sensually. At present you are in all respects right, in my eyes: that's because you reserve so very much, as I do. If you knew all about me (perhaps you do: your subtlety is very great: shall I put it 'if I knew that you knew . . .') you'd think

very little of me. And I wouldn't like to feel that I was on the way to being able to know about you. However, perhaps the unpublished novel isn't all that. You may have kept ever so much out of it. Everywhere else you write far within your strength.

This novel may yet be published and we shall see whether Forster again manifests that reserve of power, the ease, grace and mastery which evoke Keats's 'strength half-leaning on his own right arm'. To the undergraduates who ask 'Why have you written no novels since *A Passage to India*?' Forster replies 'Well, I hadn't anything more I wanted to say'. But he had a great deal more to say in other fields: criticism, biography, reviews, libretti and broadcasting.

In these other fields he frequently excels, but without showing the exquisite artistry found in his novels, especially *Howards End* and *A Passage to India*, a draft of which was nearing completion in 1913, after his first visit to India. The First World War, followed by the rise to power of the fascist dictators, the cataclysm of the Second World War, the partition of India and its subsequent agony, were world events which radically affected Forster's mind and spirit. This effect is clear in his literary output. He forsakes the novel form and gradually turns his attention to constructing a defence of western civilisation's cultural traditions. His biographies declare his roots and his affections; his criticism and broadcasting are characterised by a political pungency, which at times is so urgent in tone as to strike a note almost of panic, lest the forces of barbarism triumph.

It was Forster's belief that music is the deepest of the arts and 'deep beneath the arts'. Music more than the written word might civilise the barbarian. The *Howards End* passage which sets out the audience's reaction to Beethoven's Fifth Symphony illustrates the inadequacy of words to deal with a musical experience; but even Tibby's intellectual approach, which avoids verbalisation and concentrates on such technicalities as 'the transitional passage on the drum', is treated unsympathetically, to Benjamin Britten's dismay:

> I can't help reacting sympathetically to the boy and want to know more about him.   ASPECTS OF E. M. FORSTER, p. 84

Music plays a large part in the five novels and in the writing that follows. In the novels music has an integrating power; in subsequent essays he upholds music as part of that blessed heritage we must not lose. Rose Macaulay stresses the danger of attributing to music more power than any one art can have:

> Music can express what is inexpressible in words, words can express what is inexpressible in music; music can give backgrounds and undertones and symphonies of thought and passion, can report on the immortal real and reveal the spirit; but words can convey fragments and detail, those rich phenomenal felicities and humours which are equally the human being's outfit, and harder to get across to those who have not known the human being in the flesh.
>
> THE WRITINGS OF E. M. FORSTER, p. 258

Forster, with the introduction of his musical themes, with his patterned and rhythmic evocations—the wasp, for instance, in *A Passage to India*—is attempting to express the inexpressible. Godbole, who directs the music at the Gokul Ashtami festival, evokes through the images of the rhythm, Mrs. Moore, a wasp and the stone to which it clung. Forster's doctrine here, as Malcolm Bradbury discovers

> ... is, of course, a species of transcendence, a momentary vision of the whole, the invocation of a universe invested with spirit. It links up with the symbolist plot of the novel, its power as a radiant image, rather than with plot in the linear sense, with its world of 'and then ... and then ...' Threading its way through the novel, to an old woman and a wasp, it takes these 'soliciting images' and puts them in a new association—not with all things, but with each other and with what else comes almost unbidden into the world of spirit. ... Things, in freeing themselves from their traditional associations, social and historical, form a new order, beyond dialogue, beyond human plot, in the realm where poetic figures function on their own order of consciousness.
>
> ASPECTS OF E. M. FORSTER, 140–41

Music and mysticism are means of transcendence, and in Forster's work they are often closely allied. Virginia Woolf believes that he is 'always constrained to build the cage-society, in all its intricacy and triviality, before he can free the prisoner'.

Sawston is clearly the caged society of *Where Angels Fear to Tread* and *The Longest Journey*. In *A Room with a View* Lucy Honeychurch's cage is a self-deception which persuades her to accept second-hand criteria. The pregnant Helen Schlegel in *Howards End* is hunted down but not caged. She is set free by Leonard Bast's death, which has all the significance of a sacrificial symbol. In *A Passage to India* we are confronted by blocked passages, incommunicable bridge parties, and even the despair of personal relations as a means of bringing the races closer to each other. Escape from this cage is no easy matter. Hints of transcendence are in the strange telepathic understanding between some of the characters, in the elements of universality expressed so differently through the echo in the caves and the birth of Shri Krishna in the temple, and in the overarching sky which dominates both Chandrapore and the civil station, and which reaches as far as the fists and fingers of the Marabar Hills.

Virginia Woolf, in a tetchy and ungenerous review of Forster's work, states that both *Howards End* and *A Passage to India* fail as works of art because the author is unable to build the rainbow bridge between prose and passion. She analyses the problem he sets himself as follows:

> It is the soul that matters; and the soul, as we have seen, is caged in a solid villa of red brick somewhere in the suburbs of London. It seems then that if his books are to succeed in their mission his reality must at certain points become irradiated; his brick must be lit up; we must see the whole building saturated with light. We have at once to believe in the complete reality of the suburb and in the complete reality of the soul. In this combination of realism and mysticism his closest affinity is, perhaps, with Ibsen. Ibsen has the same realistic power. A room is to him a room, a writing table a writing table, and a waste-paper basket a waste-paper basket. At the same time, the paraphernalia of reality have at certain moments to become the veil through which we see infinity.

THE DEATH OF THE MOTH, pp. 144-5

She believes this failure is attributable to Forster, with his outstanding gift for observation, recording too much and too literally. The great scenes fail, she thinks, because of the author's self-conscious ambiguity. The bookcase falling on Leonard Bast should come down upon him 'with all the dead weight of a smoke-dried culture'.

The analogy with Ibsen is misleading. It is true both authors write with a poet's vision, reality and mysticism merge; but it is precisely because Forster is a novelist rather than a dramatist that there is such detail and complexity in the background presentation. Leonard Bast's semi-basement in Camelia Road and Aziz's fly-blown room are masterpieces of descriptive detail. Forster's end is certainly more discursive, more ambiguous than Ibsen's; above all he is not concerned with tragic issues. Hedda takes her father's pistol and shoots herself through the temple. Her quest for heroism has been in vain; she must kill herself and her unborn child. Leonard Bast, struck over the shoulders with the flat of a sword, dies of a heart attack. As he falls he pulls the bookcase on top of him. It is not heroic; it is not tragic. Helen gives birth to Leonard's child, who with the Schlegels inherits Howards End and fair prospects of happiness. Ibsen's gloomy genius transmutes reality in a flash, and we see the dark forces that threaten man's fulfilment. Forster is no less aware of these forces, but his methods of revealing them are tragi-comic; cheerfulness keeps bursting in. He is at one with Jane Austen when she says, 'Let other pens dwell on guilt and misery'; and it is because of his irrepressible humour that he will neither join the prophet-novelists, revered in *Aspects of the Novel*, nor wholly satisfy Virginia Woolf, who is looking for a greater solemnity than Forster's genre intends. High seriousness is there, but it is to stress the coexistence of prose and passion, rather than the transmutation of prose into passion.

Forster has been criticised for being spinsterly in his treatment of physical love. It is true that only one work records the happy consummation of sexual love, *A Room with a View*, but all his novels and most of his short stories are concerned with this aspect of human relationship. On examination it becomes immediately clear that the happy achievement of physical love is a rarity. Rickie, in *The Longest Journey*, had witnessed the passionate embrace of Gerald and Agnes. 'The sight burnt into his brain' and created in him an extraordinary exaltation, but when married to Agnes himself, he reaps nothing but frustration, contempt, and a crippled child that mercifully dies. Impotence is the lot of Kuno when he tries to escape from the Time Machine; Harcourt Worters, in 'Other Kingdom', fails to possess Miss Beauchamp who, dryad-like, rather than relinquish her freedom, turns into a beech tree. In *Where Angels Fear to Tread*, paternity rather than sexual passion proves the more powerful emotion. Caroline Abbott loves Gino passionately, but until she is in a railway carriage well on her way to England, she does not reveal her love. Gino will never know, but Philip Herriton is told at a moment when he himself, stirring from years of atrophied feeling, is about to declare himself a warm devotee of Miss Abbott.

Have then Forster's writings at their heart a study of separation rather than connection? *Howards End* stresses the gulf which divides classes and minds. Physical love in that novel proves an inadequate bridge. Adela, in *A Passage to India*, goes to India to marry Ronny. She returns to England a spinster having played the principal role in a scandal that savagely set alight the racial issues in Chandrapore and beyond. During Mrs. Moore's visit to the caves Adela's marriage to Ronny is reduced to a matter of little significance:

> She felt increasingly (vision or nightmare?) that, though people are important, the relations between them are not, and that in particular too much fuss has been made over marriage: centuries of carnal embracement, yet man is no nearer to understanding man. And today she felt this with such force that it seemed itself a relationship, itself a person who was trying to take hold of her hand.   PI 141

Fielding marries Stella, Mrs. Moore's daughter, and although the union, we learn, is 'blessed', there is an apparent imbalance between Fielding's passion and Stella's remoteness. The blurring of this sexual relationship is deliberate, but puzzling. The symbols are no longer acting as signposts.

The symbolic significance of the cave is not obscured. One of the signposts reads 'womb', the innermost meeting place of man and woman; but despite all the furore that ensues, it becomes evident that Adela imagined she was assaulted, and that Aziz did not even set foot in the same cave. This crucial non-meeting of man and woman, East and West, bears also a non-sexual interpretation. Through repeated references to Jung, whom Forster never read, Wilfred Stone, in his book *The Cave and the Mountain*, urges us to accept that

> the novel asks us to be responsible, to integrate ourselves, to link reason and instinct, to base our civilised arrangements on what the human race has in common instead of on what rives it into races, classes, religions, sexes, and divided personalities.

The non-meeting in the cave certainly was the occasion, in Adela and others, of bringing the conscious and unconscious into contact and, although it raised a storm of prejudice and passion, the barriers are more clearly defined as not external but in the mind. There is more here than sexual curiosity or sexual satisfaction. Stone quotes Jung to effect:

> Separation from his instinctual nature inevitably plunges civilised man into the conflict between conscious and unconscious, spirit and nature, knowledge and faith, a split that becomes pathological the moment his consciousness is no longer able to neglect or suppress his instinctual side.

The mating or failure to mate of Forster's characters may be interpreted symbolically. In *Howards End* and *A Passage to India* we encounter, in high seriousness, the failure in man to integrate the prose and passion in his life, and the failure of classes, ideologies and races to overcome their prejudices. In a much lighter vein, in *A Room with a View*, the impossibility of an alliance between the Middle Ages and the first stirrings of the Renaissance is wonderfully epitomised in that unhappy embrace which Cecil Vyse offers Lucy Honeychurch. His gold pince-nez is dislodged and flattened between them. Mr. Beebe is quick to detect in Cecil Vyse sufficient of the medieval ascetic temperament to realise that his instinctual side is towards celibacy. Lucy, on the other hand, is lifted out of her medievalism, with its close observation of the social hierarchy and its inhibition of any unguarded or passionate response, by George's demonstrative love for her. The murder of the Italian in the Piazza Signoria is a flashback to renaissance Florence. His blood splashes on to Lucy's photographs, and so George throws them into the Arno. When she and George lean on a parapet overlooking the river, Lucy realises that George lacks chivalry, courtesy and a sense of awe. In fact he is anything but medieval. But she has been in his arms, and she is beginning to recognise the sound of her own blood-beat. The chapter ends

> Leaning her elbows on the parapet, she contemplated the River Arno, whose roar was suggesting some unexpected melody to her ears.

The Renaissance has claimed her.

Lucy Honeychurch resolves her conflict before marriage. Rickie Elliot is less fortunate. By nature a celibate, he is seduced by a siren; and an inner conflict develops with pathological results. 'It is better to marry than to burn' St. Paul had written. Sexually Forster's characters do not burn fiercely, but for many of them, and Rickie Elliot is one, they would do better to burn than to marry.

ASPECTS OF STYLE

Forster thinks highly of plot, poorly of story. In *Aspects of the Novel* he distinguishes between them in this way:

> We have defined a story as a narrative of events arranged in their time-sequence. A plot is also a narrative of events, the emphasis falling on causality. 'The king died and then the queen died' is a story. 'The king died and then the queen died of grief' is a plot.
>
> AN 116

He himself is such an excellent story-teller that it seems strange that he should be one of those who regretfully agree 'Yes—oh dear yes—the novel tells a story'. It is true that his artistry is at its highest when he lays his plots, which contain many carefully laid clues which may be picked up later in the novel's development. This is one reason why rereading Forster's novels can be so rewarding. The subtlety of his plot-structure sometimes escapes a first reading. There are rarely any unaccountable loose ends. On the other hand, where a character in the story is not essential for the development of the plot, he can be rapidly dispatched, with callous abruptness. 'Gerald died that afternoon. He was broken up in the football match.' Neither story nor plot make further demands on Gerald, and so Gerald must die. In his maturer work there are the sudden deaths of Ruth Wilcox and Mrs. Moore, but these ladies exert their influence on the plot long after their demise. Death and marriage are such prominent features of the Victorian novel, but in Forster's work they are relegated to a position of little significance. For example, Chapter X in *Howards End* comes to an end with the Wilcox family happily united at King's Cross Station. Chapter XI begins 'The funeral was over'. We are to gather that Ruth Wilcox has died. Marriages are dealt with as summarily. The fuller treatment given to Evie's wedding in *Howards End* is to make it a focal point, not for the nuptials, but for Margaret to be confronted by the bores and the brutes of Henry Wilcox's colonial set, and for Helen to face Henry Wilcox with his past, in the person of Mrs. Bast.

With the exception of *A Room with a View* none of the novels concludes with a happy marriage. Marriage does not seem to contain the answer to the questions which the author raises. We recall Mrs. Moore regretting those fruitless centuries of carnal embracement. More is needed than marriage to heal the world's wounds.

Within Forster's stories, time, place and characters adhere. The seasons, for instance, play a prominent part in each of the novels. In *A Room with a View* Lucy Honeychurch is kissed by George among the spring violets, which are in such profusion that they seem to her to run down from the hill-side 'in rivulets and streams and cataracts'. When she notices George, he is standing at the brink of this pool of violets, 'like a swimmer who prepares'. Their embrace is disturbed by a call from Miss Bartlett, 'who stood brown against the view'. The next occasion on which Lucy meets George is an autumn day in Surrey. George, together with Freddy and Mr. Beebe, has been swimming in the rain-filled pool in the woods near Summer Street. With youthful exuberance, naked apart from wearing Mr. Beebe's hat, George, who has been whooping among the trees, suddenly comes upon Lucy, her mother and Cecil Vyse. This autumn dip puts new heart into George, and with a fresh resolution to win for himself the woman he loves, it is not surprising that the following spring we read that he and Lucy, now married, have returned to Florence to share that room with a view.

The three parts of *A Passage to India*, Mosque, Caves, Temple, catch India's three main seasonal moods. In the temperate weather in the first part, overtures of friendship are made, not without success; when the hot weather comes in the second part it precipitates the crisis and the separation; in the third part the coming of the monsoon falls at the same time as the birth of Shri Krishna, and at this juncture of the festival Fielding, Aziz, Mrs. Moore's children and Professor Godbole find themselves close to each other in the warm shallow water.

In *Howards End* Margaret Schlegel lays autumn flowers on Ruth Wilcox's winter grave, and the frost withers them before morning. These tawny chrysanthemums have seemed to the Wilcoxes so inappropriate. At the very end of the book, when Ruth Wilcox has had her way, and Howards End has passed to Margaret Schlegel, it is mid-summer; the scythe is at work in the hay-field.

> The meadow was being recut, the great red poppies were reopening in the garden. July would follow with the little red poppies among the wheat, August with the cutting of the wheat. These events would become part of her year after year. Every summer she would fear lest the well should give out, every winter lest the pipes should freeze; every westerly gale might blow the wych-elm down and bring the end of all things, and so she could not read or talk during a westerly gale. The air was tranquil now.   HE 354-5

And that is the mood in which the novel must end—a midsummer tranquillity.

If, in these novels, the time of year frequently establishes mood, place apparently has the power to determine action, if not to alter character. Rickie Elliot, who has flourished in Cambridge, withers at Sawston; Miss Abbott, who at Sawston is a high-minded conventionally principled lady, is reduced to a state of emotional confusion in Monteriano. Ronny Heaslop, who in England had enjoyed playing the viola, blushes with shame when in India his mother refers to this accomplishment. Howards End, which gives Henry Wilcox hay-fever and where his sons, in different ways, behave shamefully, is the Schlegels' spiritual home. It is not just that their furniture fits in perfectly, but Helen and Margaret do as well. From those early days when Forster wrote 'The Road From Colonus' and 'The Story of a Panic', the *genius loci* has had strange power in his work. Nowhere is this power more deeply felt, nor more influential in the destinies of so many characters, than in the three parts of *A Passage to India*. Mosque, Caves and Temple are all places of meeting, but in none of these places can the different races meet in harmony. The very end of the novel rejects the possibility of any place on the earth or under the sky which will bring the Moslem and the Englishman together again in friendship.

It is not surprising that Forster's novels adapt so well to the stage. He has the eye of the dramatist for setting his scenes, and the ear of the dramatist for dialogue. In recalling some of the most memorable scenes in the novels, background details and dialogue coalesce. What a magnificent bustling opening to *Where Angels Fear to Tread*! Mr. Kinghorn runs up and down Charing Cross station for a foot-warmer, Mrs. Herriton snubs Mrs. Theobald, and Philip, in his ignorance, urges the feckless Lilia to love and understand the Italians. No less memorable from the same work, and infinitely more poignant, is the bathing of the baby. The reaction of the audience to the opera in this novel is a hilarious foretaste of the subtler study of the audience's reaction to a more austere work in *Howards End*. A scene epitomising the meeting and parting of two classes unable to communicate satisfactorily with each other is the occasion on which Leonard Bast calls at Wickham Place to retrieve his umbrella. In the club house at Chandrapore the classes can communicate, but prejudice has erected insurmountable barriers. In *A Passage to India* the club house and the court room scenes are superbly described in dramatic terms. The dialogue is there in all its crispness. The adapter has very little to do.

Dr. Leavis believed that in creating Leonard Bast Forster was grasping at something that lay outside his first-hand experience, and therefore was doomed to failure. Wilfred Stone also finds it difficult to take Forster seriously when he writes of Leonard Bast 'Perhaps the keenest happiness he had ever known was during a railway journey to Cambridge, where a decent-mannered undergraduate had spoken to him'. Forster was never a Cambridge recluse. When he came to write *Howards End* he was a widely-travelled man who had not confined his acquaintance within class or cultural limits. It is typical of the man that he was later to travel second class on the Indian trains so that he could mix freely with the Indians. The authenticity of Leonard Bast should be tested by the action and the dialogue. The action rings true. The critical situation is the scene at the Shropshire inn when he is overwhelmed by Helen. He is attracted to her, envious of her class and learning, tired and bored by Jacky. Credibility is more stretched by Helen's action than his. In dialogue, Bast is impeccable, from his Magnolia Road greetings to the inarticulacy of his conversation with Jacky. For those of us who have seen Tony Hancock struggling with Bertrand Russell's *History of Western Philosophy* on his bed in his flat at East Cheam, Leonard Bast's reading of Ruskin's *Stones of Venice* is not just similar to a television programme but close to life:

> 'Seven miles to the north of Venice—'
> How perfectly the famous chapter opens! How supreme its command of admonition and of poetry! The rich man is speaking to us from his gondola. . . .
> Leonard was trying to form his style on Ruskin: he understood him to be the greatest master of English prose. . . .
> Was there anything to be learnt from this fine sentence? Could he adapt it to the needs of daily life? Could he introduce it with modifications, when he wrote a letter to his brother-in-law, the lay-reader? . . .   HE 52

Forster can catch Leonard Bast's soliloquy or dialogue with such accuracy because he is a good listener, a keen observer, and his interests are certainly not confined to men and women of his own class, as Leavis's criticism implies.

His other extraordinary gift in writing dialogue is the way he can reflect through a conversation in English the gestures and intonations of foreigners. An early masterpiece in this vein is in *Where Angels Fear to Tread* when Gino and his friend, Spiridione, sip vermouth outside the Caffè Garibaldi and discuss Gino's problems with Lilia.

> 'And she is rich?'
> 'Immensely rich.'
> 'Blonde or dark?'
> 'Blonde.'
> 'Is it possible!'
> 'It pleases me very much,' said Gino simply. 'If you remember, I always desired a blonde.' Three or four men had collected and were listening. WA 57–8

Discussion of Lilia's merits and Gino's deserts is extended to the onlookers. Indelicate sentiment is couched in a formality of phrasing which characterises Italian rather than English. Gino is worried because his wife 'wishes to take solitary walks'. Spiridione solemnly suggests a solution:

> 'She needs employment. Is she a Catholic?'
> 'No.'
> 'That is a pity. She must be persuaded. It will be a great solace to her when she is alone.'
> 'I am a Catholic, but of course I never go to church.'
> 'Of course not. Still, you might take her first. That is what my brother has done with his wife in Bologna, and he has joined the Free Thinkers. He took her once or twice himself, and now she has acquired the habit and continues to go without him.' WA 61

The culmination of Forster's genius for dialogue is found in *A Passage to India*, in which he not only succeeds in showing how Ronny Heaslop apes the Collector's speech, but also how the speech of the Indians differs radically in their use of English from the Anglo-Indians. Apart from this the main Indian characters have their own peculiar speech rhythms: Panna Lal's whining sycophancy is distinguishable from Professor Godbole's circuitous, unemphatic speech; Hamidullah's maturer tone is contrasted with Aziz's impetuosity and excitement. In Oliver Stallybrass's account of the two manuscripts of *A Passage to India* (*Aspects of E. M. Forster*, 152) he points out that the later work shows a general tendency to convert narrative into dialogue. Certainly the quality of the dialogue of the published edition, with its extraordinary variety of mood, race and situation, is one of the great triumphs of this novel, and marks the peak of Forster's achievement in this field.

CHARACTERS

In the gallery of Forster's characters we meet a great many maiden ladies, a number of dominant mothers and aunts, very few fathers and uncles, but frequently, as central characters, young men with artistic leanings who find it extremely difficult to fuse the world of art with the world they live in. Mrs. Ruth Wilcox and Mrs. Moore stand apart. The author has endowed them with a mysterious power which is operative after their death. There are indications that Mrs. Moore's children, Stella and Ralph, share their mother's power. Mrs. Moore as she approaches death becomes vexatious, obstructive and downright unpleasant. Her Christian virtues fall from her, but she becomes a goddess whom the Indians can call upon, and her telepathic power continues to exert an influence on both Adela and Professor Godbole.

In most of the novels there are characters of charm, wit and physical beauty. *Howards End*, however, does not seem to have its fair share: no character is positively attractive. The Wilcoxes are brutish; the Schlegels bluestockings. In this sense *A Passage to India* is redeemed by the courage, independence and good will of Fielding, and by the charm and open-heartedness of Aziz. This gallery of portraits is painted by an artist who believed that once created his characters possessed a life of their own. The degree of his detachment is the extent of their strength.

T. E. Lawrence writing to Edward Garnet in 1924:

> . . . Hudson gone.
> Conrad gone.
> Hardy very old: G. Moore gaga; D. H. L. ditto; whom have we to welcome year by year? (Not Aldous Huxley, not a Sitwell, not J. Joyce, not Wyndham Lewis: somebody lovable.) E. M. Forster: very good; but is he quite great? I like him, but a little shame-facedly.

Forster eludes categorising. He was on the verge of the Cambridge Apostles, and involved but not a central figure in the Bloomsbury circle. His modesty and gentleness often gave rise to condescension in acquaintances. The subtlety of his art, his ability to write with detachment and passion, created an ambiguity which made the critics ill-at-ease and even T. E. Lawrence a little shamefaced. Time increases his fame, the ambiguity is accepted as a positive virtue, his vigour of mind and pursuit of truth are more fully recognised. He is no longer considered 'a Jane Austen in trousers' or a decorous Edwardian who thought writing about sex bad taste. But there is still little agreement among the critics as to which of his novels has pride of place. Lionel Trilling, for instance, declares roundly that 'Howards End is undoubtedly Forster's masterpiece', while F. R. Leavis, turning from Howards End in a state of shock and distress, recognises in A Passage to India, with many characteristic reservations, a classic: 'not only a most significant document of our age, but a truly memorable work of literature'.

It is an idle pursuit to arrange Forster's works in order of merit or to find the correct place for the author in the top twenty. Popular taste is fickle, and the most distinguished critics adopt totally different criteria. That he is great, there is no doubt: that he is greater than most of us have thought is very probable. In conclusion, the complexity of his work, his depth of insight into the human condition and his consummate artistry are reflected in the words of T. E. Lawrence who writes to Forster, having read A Passage to India:

It's a three or four-sided thing, more like sculpture, therefore, than painting. Extraordinarily satisfying, to the reader, in the multiplicity of its effect and cross-lights and bearings. . . . You can shape so spare and trim a thing out of an innumerable heap of impressions and materials. . . . Oh, it's despairingly well done.

Bibliography

The works of E. M. Forster are published by Random House (New York) and Harcourt, Brace & World (New York), except, for *Alexandria: A History and a Guide*, published by Peter Smith Inc. (Magnolia, Mass.).

CRITICAL WORKS

Bradbury, Malcolm, ed. *'Forster'. A Collection of Critical Essays* (Prentice-Hall, Inc., Englewood Cliffs, New Jersey, 1966).

Brander, L. *E. M. Forster: A Critical Study* (Hillary House Publishers, New York).

Colmer, John. *E. M. Forster: 'A Passage to India'* (Barron's Educational Series, Inc., Woodbury, N.Y.).

Holroyd, Michael. *Lytton Strachey*, Volume 1 (Holt, Rinehart & Winston, Inc., New York).

Lawrence, T. E. *Selected Letters*, ed. David Garnett (Viking Press, New York).

Leavis, F. R. *The Common Pursuit* (New York Univ. Press, New York, 1964).

Macaulay, Rose. *The Writings of E. M. Forster* (Folcroft Press, Folcroft, Pa.).

Stallybrass, Oliver, ed. *Aspects of E. M. Forster*. Essays and Recollections written for his Ninetieth Birthday, 1st January, 1969 (Harcourt, Brace & World, New York).

Stone, Wilfred. *The Cave and the Mountain. A Study of E. M. Forster* (Stanford Univ. Press, Stanford, California).

Trilling, Lionel. *E. M. Forster* (New Directions, New York).

Warner, Rex. *E. M. Forster* (British Book Center, Elmsford, N.Y.).

Woolf, Leonard. *Sowing. An Autobiography of the Years 1880–1904* (Harcourt, Brace & World, New York).

Woolf, Virginia. *Captain's Death Bed & Other Essays* (Harcourt, Brace & World).

Woolf, Virginia. *Contemporary Writers* (Harcourt, Brace & World, New York).

Index

Index to E. M. Forster's Works

Main entries are indicated by heavy type

Stay On Top of Your Classwork with
ARCO'S 1,000 IDEAS FOR TERM PAPER SERIES

Concise yet thorough guides to the planning and preparation of term papers for high school and college students—how to plan the paper, how and where to find research sources, how to organize the project, how to select a topic. $1.95 each, except where noted.

1,000 IDEAS FOR TERM PAPERS IN:

AMERICAN HISTORY
From pre-revolutionary times to the post-World War II period.

ECONOMICS
From macroeconomic theory to the literature of Smith, Marx, Keynes.

ENGLISH
From Chaucer to modern realism. **1.45**

SOCIAL SCIENCE
Topics on psychology, anthropology, sociology and political science.

SOCIOLOGY
Communications, war, urbanization, family, criminology, research design, analysis of data.

WORLD LITERATURE
From Beowulf to the twentieth century.

All books are available at your bookseller or directly from ARCO PUBLISHING CO. INC., 219 Park Avenue South, New York, N.Y. 10003. Send price of books plus 25¢ postage and handling. Sorry no C.O.D.